THE CREATIVE COOK

A Mediterranean

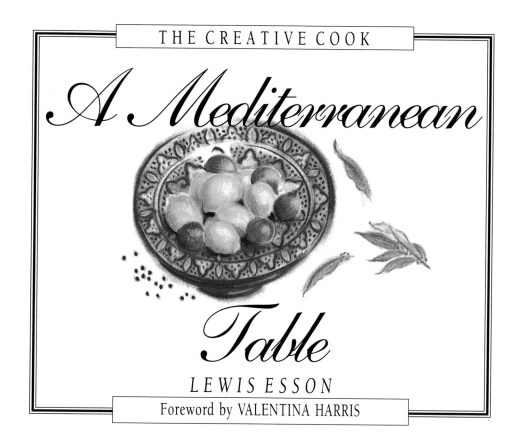

Table

LEWIS ESSON

Foreword by VALENTINA HARRIS

COLE
GROUP

In memory of Colin Clark, who taught me how
useful it was to "have spaghetti up your sleeve"

Please note the following:

Quantities given in all the recipes serve 4 people unless otherwise stated.

Butter and margarine are packaged in a variety of forms, including 1-pound blocks and ¼-pound sticks. A stick equals 8 tablespoons (½ cup).

Cream used is specified as light cream (containing from 18 percent to 30 percent milk fat), whipping cream (30 percent to 36 percent milk fat), or heavy cream (at least 36 percent milk fat).

Flour used is all-purpose flour, unless otherwise specified.

Preparation of ingredients, such as the cleaning, trimming, and peeling of vegetables and fruit, is presumed and the text refers to any aspect of this only if unusual, such as onions used unpeeled, etc.

Citrus fruit should be thoroughly washed to remove any agricultural residues. For this reason, whenever a recipe uses the rind of any citrus such as oranges, lemon, or limes, the text specifies washed fruit. Wash the fruit thoroughly, rinse well, and pat dry. If using organically grown fruit, rinse briefly and pat dry.

Eggs used are large unless otherwise specified. Because of the risk of contamination with salmonella bacteria, current recommendations from health professionals are that children, pregnant women, people on immuno-suppressant drugs, and the elderly should not eat raw or lightly cooked eggs. This book includes recipes with raw and lightly cooked eggs. These recipes are marked by an ★ in the text.

Editorial Direction: Lewis Esson Publishing
Art Director: Mary Evans
Design: Peter Butler
Illustrations: Alison Barratt
Food for Photography: Meg Jansz
Styling: Jackie Boase
Editorial Assistant: Penny David
American Editor: Norma MacMillan
Production: Julia Golding

Text copyright © Lewis Esson 1993
Foreword copyright © Valentina Harris 1993
Photography copyright © Julie Fisher 1993
Design and layout copyright © Conran Octopus 1993

Published by Cole Group
4415 Sonoma Highway/PO Box 4089
Santa Rosa, CA 95402–4089
(707) 538–0492   FAX (707) 538–0497

First published in 1992 by
Conran Octopus Limited,
37 Shelton Street, London WC2H 9HN

A	B	C	D	E	F	G	H
3	4	5	6	7	8	9	0

ISBN 1–56426–650–8
Library of Congress Cataloguing in process

Typeset by Servis Filmsetting Ltd
Printed in Hong Kong

Distributed to the book trade by Publishers Group West

CONTENTS

FOREWORD

As I write this, the rain is dripping miserably out of a dull, gray sky. It is supposed to be summer here, but the air is as chilled, damp, and cold as it is in mid-November. Homesickness for the warm embrace of my homeland sweeps through me. I long to be strolling around a noisy Sicilian street market, where the sunlight bounces off the brilliant reds, yellows, greens, and purples of the piles of glorious juicy produce; where the smells of freshly brewed espresso and baking bread and brioches come wafting out of every café doorway that I pass.

I'd like to join in with the early preparation of the vineyards for the summer heat. And when I'm hot and sweaty from the morning's toil (because spring in Sicily is completely different from the wintry scene in my garden!), I'd like to sit under a cool pergola, where I would settle down to the important business of feeding my body, but most especially my soul, with a plate of pasta dressed with a fragrantly scented, deliciously rich sauce, and then savor the fishermen's morning catch that has just come off the wonderfully chaotic, brightly painted wooden smacks. This would be accompanied by mounds of vegetables grown to an incredible size and level of perfection on the nearby volcanic slopes of Mount Etna. Then crusty bread drizzled with deep-green olive oil (just to wipe my plate quite clean) and fresh ewes' milk cheeses, and huge perfumed fruit . . .

Perhaps it would be more constructive to prepare my own feast, right here and now. A trip to the local supermarket cannot quite replace the passion and fervor of the midday pitch in a Sicilian street market, but the variety of flavors, colors, and textures and the sheer availability have improved immeasurably over the last few years. I am delighted to be able to fill my kitchen with the scent of fresh basil, to drizzle olive oil over the garlic-rubbed slices of ciabatta bread, to slice into a mozzarella that is freshly made today – with the secure knowledge that there is plenty more where that came from, just nearby!

Books like *A Mediterranean Table* help to banish these cold days and bring to life the riches of the food treasures of my homeland. In the summer – provided the weather permits you to indulge in *al fresco* eating – this wonderful and comprehensive book will help you to create a complete Mediterranean feast. The recipes contained in this book are not specifically Italian or Spanish or Greek. They simply celebrate the joy and warmth of the Mediterranean and allow you to bask in its many seductive pleasures. I am delighted that the ingredients and the recipes are at last so readily accessible that the magic of the region can weave a spell on you, so that in the time it takes to boil the pasta it can transport you to the sights, scents, and sounds of *A Mediterranean Table* . . .

VALENTINA HARRIS

INTRODUCTION

The Mediterranean region embraces a wide and diverse area from the more familiar shores of Spain, Southern France, and Italy to the farther-flung territories of Turkey, the Middle East, and North Africa.

However, the food of all these richly varied countries and cultures does have some very strong similarities. The warm temperate climate in the area produces an abundance of vegetables, fruits, nuts, and grains that form the heart of Mediterranean cuisine. As a result there is simply not the same emphasis on meat and dairy produce as is so prevalent in the American diet. Instead, olive oil is the favored cooking medium and meat is considered much more as just another flavoring ingredient rather than as the mainstay of each and every meal.

As well as giving dishes that are gloriously flavorsome, this very different emphasis also has the advantage of producing food that is much more in line with current thinking on healthy eating. Not only is there far less saturated fat and a better supply of fiber and complex carbohydrates in Mediterranean food, but it is rich in what are now sometimes known as the "superfoods." These are not only better for you but are becoming recognized as having very potent properties in the prevention of illness and the lengthening of active life.

For instance, olive oil is one of the richest sources of monounsaturated fats, which are now thought to have an even more beneficial effect on blood cholesterol levels than the much-vaunted polyunsaturated fats, and they help combat cancer at the same time. The same is true of the oily fish, such as sardines, mackerel, and tuna, so abundant in the Mediterranean. Moreover, the deep-colored vegetables and fruits of the region, notably tomatoes, zucchini, broccoli, spinach, and watercress and mangoes, melons, apricots, and oranges, have high levels of vitamins C and E and beta-carotene, which are now also credited with similar properties. Even the garlic so prevalent in Mediterranean food has a long history of health-giving powers that have recently been substantiated by medical science: It would seem to reduce blood cholesterol and blood pressure and also help prevent the formation of blood clots.

Much Mediterranean food is now well established as part of our own culinary scene. Over the years, enterprising immigrant restaurateurs and the effect of increased international travel have made items like pizzas and pasta part of our everyday diet.

The increasingly multi-cultural nature of our society has also brought items like fresh coriander (cilantro) and a wonderful array of exotic fruit and vegetables to our markets, and a remarkable range of legumes, spices, and flavorings like rose and orange flower water to our specialty stores.

Today's emphasis on healthier diet and vegetarianism has also brought more exotic dishes like *hummus*, *couscous*, and *tabbouleh* increasingly into our consciousness. As a result, most of the necessary ingredients are now readily available to us.

For instance, many supermarket shelves now display a range of olive oils almost as wide as that of their wines. This is one area in which it is worth spending some money: Generally speaking, the better the quality of the olive oil you use, the better the dish will taste – and this is every bit as true when the oil is cooked as when it is used in dressings! Always buy extra virgin oil, which is produced by the first cold pressing of the olives. It should have a fine clear golden or slightly greeny color and a rich nutty flavor. Like wines, try many different types until you establish your favorite. If the cost concerns you, remember that two or three spoonfuls of even the most expensive of olive oils works out very cheaply indeed compared to many other less influential ingredients in a dish.

One thing that can be difficult to come by fresh is the rich, ripe plum tomato that is central to so many Mediterranean dishes, especially pasta sauces. Some plum tomatoes that do reach our markets may be pale, fibrous objects with little of the robust flavor of their sun-ripened Mediterranean counterparts. For this reason, it can often be preferable to use a quality brand of canned plum tomato, which will give a better approximation of the real tomato taste.

Fresh herbs, especially mint, coriander (cilantro), basil, chervil, chives, thyme, and rosemary, are so much part of the unique character of Mediterranean food that it is always worth the extra effort and expense of obtaining them – after all, so many are now available from our supermarkets either in bunches or growing in tiny pots. Remember, too, that whenever parsley is called for in a recipe it would normally be the flat-leaf or Italian variety more common in that part of the world. The flavor of flat-leaf parsley is distinctly different from the more familiar curly version. Fortunately flat-leaf parsley is now widely available in this country, and once you have tried it I guarantee you will seek out its taste more often.

It is, after all, taste that distinguishes Mediterranean food. The intense flavors of the freshest of sun-drenched vegetables and fruits, combined in interesting and unusual ways with aromatic herbs and pungent spices, local cheeses, nuts, and other subtle flavorings, produce enticing, colorful, and mouthwatering meals for all occasions.

SOUPS, APPETIZERS, AND MEZZE

*I*n many Mediterranean countries a wide variety of small snacks and tidbits is an important part of the culinary tradition, like *tapas* in Spain and *mezze* in Greece, Turkey, and the Middle East. As simple as a bowl of olives or a dip, or as complex as grape leaves or phyllo pastries filled with all manner of stuffings, they are served all through the day in cafés and bars. A common practice is to start a meal with a selection of such dishes, and to follow this with a plainly cooked piece of fish or meat – or even just a salad. Sometimes an entire meal is composed of such dishes. The abundance of good vegetables grown in the region has also made substantial soups a common meal in themselves, often topped with a thick highly-flavored sauce, and served with good crusty bread.

Clockwise from the left: Pissaladière (page 10), Crostini with Wild Mushrooms (page 11), and Bruschette with Tomatoes (page 10)

PISSALADIÈRE

SERVES 4

FOR THE DOUGH

1 ½ tsp active dry yeast
1 ⅔ cups flour, plus more for dusting
1 egg, lightly beaten
½ tsp salt
1 tbsp olive oil

FOR THE TOPPING

5 tbsp olive oil
2 ¼ lb onions, very thinly sliced
3 garlic cloves, minced
1 bay leaf
1 tsp chopped fresh thyme leaves or ½ tsp dried thyme
1 tsp chopped fresh basil or ½ tsp dried basil
1 tsp chopped fresh rosemary or ½ tsp dried rosemary
salt and freshly ground black pepper
3 tbsp red wine
1 tbsp capers, drained and mashed
1 cup canned plum tomatoes, drained and chopped
24 canned anchovy fillets, drained and cut in half lengthwise
24 small pitted black olives

PISSALADIÈRES, a speciality of the Provence region of France, are flat, open tarts not dissimilar to Italian pizzas.

First make the dough: Dissolve the yeast in ⅓ cup of warm water. Sift the flour into a warm bowl and form a well in the center of it.

When the yeast mixture is spongy, pour it into the middle of the well together with the egg and salt. Gradually mix in the flour from the edges until the mixture forms a smooth dough.

Turn it onto a floured surface and knead until smooth and elastic, about 5 minutes.

Generously grease a bowl with the oil, place the ball of dough in it, and turn the ball to coat it thoroughly with the oil. Cover with a damp cloth and let rise in a warm place until it has risen to about twice its original bulk, about 1 hour.

Meanwhile make the topping: Put 4 tablespoons of oil in a large frying pan (preferably with a lid) over medium heat and add the onions, garlic, bay leaf, and other herbs. Season well and cook until the onions are translucent, about 5 minutes. Add the wine, capers, and tomatoes. Stir well, cover, and cook over low heat until the onions are very soft, about 30 minutes longer.

Preheat the oven to 475°F and grease a 10-inch pie or pizza pan, or a baking sheet, with a little of the remaining olive oil.

Remove the risen dough from the bowl and knead it briefly on a lightly floured surface. Then roll it out and use it to line the pie or pizza pan, or simply press it into the pan so that it is higher at the edges and there is a hollow in the center. Alternatively, form the dough into such a round container on the prepared baking sheet.

Adjust the seasoning of the onion mixture and spoon it into the center of the pie, leaving a broad rim around the edge. Using the strips of anchovy, make a lattice pattern on top of the filling and press the olives into the spaces between. Brush the uncovered rim with the remaining olive oil. Let the pissaladière rise in a warm place, about 15 minutes.

Bake until the dough is crisp and brown, 20–25 minutes. Serve hot or warm.

NOTE: Defrosted frozen bread dough, pizza dough, or pie pastry also works well in this recipe.

BRUSCHETTE WITH TOMATOES

SERVES 4

2 flat loaves of Italian bread (ciabatta)
2 large garlic cloves, minced
¼ cup extra virgin olive oil
4 large, very ripe tomatoes, halved
salt and freshly ground black pepper
tiny basil or tarragon leaves, for garnish (optional)

Preheat the broiler.

Split each loaf in half lengthwise (start by cutting the crusts with a knife, but try to pry the halves apart and not to slice all through cleanly, as it is necessary to create a rough surface). Then cut each of these pieces crosswise in half.

Toast the pieces of bread under the broiler, rough sides uppermost, until just beginning to brown.

While the bread is still very warm, spread each piece with some minced garlic, brush generously with oil, and then rub a tomato half all over the surface to spread the tomato pulp on it. Season well.

Return to the broiler briefly just to warm through and then garnish with the herbs, if using.

BRESAOLA WITH LEMON MUSTARD VINAIGRETTE

SERVES 4

2 washed lemons
⅓ cup extra virgin olive oil
2 tsp English mustard
salt and freshly ground black pepper
20 slices of bresaola
2 tbsp minced fresh flat-leaf parsley
about 12 tiny cherry tomatoes, for garnish
radicchio leaves, for garnish

Finely grate 2 teaspoons of zest from one of the lemons and extract 1 tablespoon of its juice. Cut the other lemon into wedges.

In a small bowl, blend the lemon zest and juice with the oil, mustard, and seasoning to taste.

Fan the slices of beef decoratively on a plate. Just before serving, mix the dressing together well again and drizzle it over the slices of beef.

Sprinkle with the parsley, garnish with the cherry tomatoes nestling in radicchio leaves, and serve with the lemon wedges.

CROSTINI WITH WILD MUSHROOMS

SERVES 4

4 tbsp extra virgin olive oil
4 garlic cloves, minced
½ lb mixed fresh wild mushrooms, preferably including some cèpes, sliced
3 tbsp lemon juice
2 tbsp chopped fresh flat-leaf parsley
salt and freshly ground black pepper
8 thick slices of crusty white Italian bread
1 tbsp anchovy paste
1 buffalo or fresh mozzarella cheese, thinly sliced
cayenne pepper

Preheat the broiler or the oven to 350°F.

In a large frying pan, heat 2 tablespoons of the oil over medium heat and sauté the garlic gently until translucent. Add the mushroom slices and sauté over medium-high heat until the mushrooms are just beginning to give off their liquid.

Increase the heat and cook briskly 3–4 minutes until the liquid has evaporated and the mushrooms are beginning to brown. Stir in the lemon juice and most of the parsley. Season with salt.

Meanwhile lightly toast the slices of bread under the broiler or in the oven.

Spread the toasted slices of bread sparingly with the anchovy paste and then brush them with the remaining oil. Spoon the sautéed mushroom mixture in heaps in the center, reserving some of the better-looking mushroom slices for garnish.

Cover the mushrooms with slices of mozzarella and sprinkle some pepper over the cheese. Broil or bake until the cheese is bubbling.

Garnish with the reserved mushrooms and parsley and dust lightly with cayenne before serving piping hot.

BRESAOLA is a specialty of Italy's Lombardy province. Best quality beef is sliced very thinly and air-cured. It is available from Italian groceries.

BRUSCHETTE could be described as Italian garlic bread while CROSTINI are more like a type of toasted sandwich.

If fresh wild mushrooms are difficult to obtain, use equal parts button mushrooms, oyster mushrooms or fresh shiitake, and dried cèpes (porcini), soaked in warm water 20 minutes.

MINESTRONE VERDE WITH PESTO

SERVES 8

¼ cup dried navy beans, soaked overnight and drained
5 garlic cloves, 2 whole, 3 minced
1 piece of salted pork rind or 2 thick slices of bacon,
diced
3 tbsp olive oil
2 small leeks, thinly sliced
2 celery stalks, with their leaves, chopped
3 tbsp chopped fresh flat-leaf parsley
1 tbsp chopped fresh basil
salt and freshly ground black pepper
½ lb fine green beans, cut into 1-inch pieces
½ cup shelled fresh green peas
2 small zucchini, cut into thick strips about 1-inch long
1 small head of green cabbage, shredded
1 large potato, finely diced
1 cup canned plum tomatoes, chopped
3 oz vermicelli
2 tbsp chopped fresh chives
freshly grated Parmesan cheese, for serving

FOR THE PESTO

1 cup packed fresh basil leaves
2 garlic cloves
½ cup pine nuts
6 tbsp freshly grated Parmesan cheese
3 tbsp extra virgin olive oil

Rinse the soaked beans and simmer them in unsalted boiling water with the whole garlic cloves and the pork skin or bacon until they are just beginning to become tender, about 2 hours. Drain and discard the garlic and pork skin or bacon.

In a large heavy pot, heat the oil over low heat. Add the leeks, minced garlic, the celery, half the parsley, and the basil. Season generously and cook until all the ingredients are soft but not browned.

Add 5 cups of warm water together with the

navy beans and remaining vegetables including the tomatoes with their juice. Bring to a boil and simmer gently until all the vegetables are tender.

Meanwhile, make the pesto: Pound the basil leaves with the garlic and pine nuts in a mortar with a pestle. Add the cheese a little at a time, pounding until the mixture is a thick paste. Then mix in the oil a little at a time, making sure it is entirely incorporated before adding any more. The finished sauce should have the consistency of creamed butter.

A few minutes before serving, crush the vermicelli into small pieces and add to the soup. When these are just tender, stir in the remaining parsley and the chives.

Serve with a little pesto swirled on top of each serving and pass the Parmesan separately.

AVGOLEMONO★

SERVES 4

5 cups chicken or vegetable stock
3 garlic cloves
⅔ cup long-grain rice
3 eggs
(★see page 2 for advice on eggs)
juice of 2 large lemons
salt and freshly ground black pepper
2 very thin lemon slices, halved, for garnish
¼ cup chopped fresh flat-leaf parsley, for garnish

Bring the stock to a boil and add the garlic cloves and rice. Simmer until the rice is just tender, about 15 minutes. Remove and discard the garlic.

Just before serving, beat the eggs lightly and then beat in some of the lemon juice until the mixture is pale and foaming. Stir a ladleful of the hot stock into the egg mixture, beating constantly. Then return the mixture to the remaining stock, stirring con-

stantly. Almost immediately remove the stock from the heat: The soup must not boil or the eggs will curdle.

Adjust the seasoning with salt and pepper and add just enough of the remaining lemon juice to give the soup a good, sharp taste. Garnish with the lemon slices and chopped parsley and serve.

AVGOLEMONO is a classic Greek soup, flavored with eggs and lemons. When the egg and lemon juice mixture is added, the soup thickens to a rich, creamy texture. The delicate flavor depends on using a good stock, preferably homemade, and on careful seasoning.

Now familiar all over the world, the Middle-Eastern chickpea purée, Hummus, *traditionally appears on most mezze tables. Such purées may simply be flavored with garlic and salt, or – as here – with lemon juice, cumin, and tahini paste, made from crushed sesame seeds, to give a fine nutty flavor. The earthy taste of tahini is also essential to the classic Turkish eggplant dip,* Baba Ghanouj. *The eggplants must first be charred to impart the right degree of smokiness. Serve both these dips with strips of pita bread or crudités, such as celery sticks, sticks of cucumber and zucchini, and sweet pepper strips.*

SPICY HUMMUS WITH TAHINI

SERVES 4

1¼ cups dried chickpeas (garbanzos), soaked overnight,
or 2½ cups canned chickpeas, drained
3 or 4 large garlic cloves, minced
juice of 3 lemons
3 tbsp extra virgin olive oil
2 tsp ground cumin
salt
cayenne pepper
⅔ cup tahini paste
2 tbsp minced fresh flat-leaf parsley
1 tbsp toasted pine nuts, for garnish (optional)
pita bread, cut into strips, for serving

Rinse the chickpeas thoroughly (carefully removing any debris and shed skins). Cover the chickpeas with water, bring to a boil, and simmer them until quite tender: just over 1 hour for dried chickpeas and only 10–15 minutes for canned chickpeas.

Drain thoroughly, reserving a little of the liquid, and purée the chickpeas in a food processor or mash them in a bowl. Add the garlic, lemon juice, 2 or 3 tablespoons of the cooking liquid, 1 tablespoon of oil, 1 teaspoon of cumin, a generous pinch of salt, and a pinch of cayenne.

Add most of the tahini and mix again to a thick, creamy consistency. Adjust the consistency, if necessary, with more tahini, cooking liquid or lemon juice. Adjust the seasoning with salt and cayenne. Turn the mixture into a shallow serving dish. Mix the remaining oil with a pinch of cayenne and a pinch of the remaining cumin. Drizzle this over the top of the hummus.

Sprinkle with the parsley and decorate with the remaining cumin and some more cayenne (a star pattern is traditional). Dot with the pine nuts, if using. Serve with pita strips or crudités.

BABA GHANOUJ

SERVES 4

2–3 large eggplants
3 large garlic cloves, minced
1 small onion, grated
salt
pinch of paprika
juice of 2 large lemons
7 tbsp tahini paste
2 tsp minced fresh mint, coriander (cilantro), or flat-leaf
parsley, for garnish
tiny pitted black olives, for garnish
1 tbsp olive oil, for serving
pita bread or crudités, for serving

Preheat the broiler or the oven to 450°F.

Either broil the eggplants, turning them regularly, or bake them in the oven, until the skins are black and blistered, about 30 minutes.

Let them cool slightly and then peel off the charred skin. Rinse the eggplants and squeeze them firmly to extract their bitter juices.

Chop the eggplant flesh coarsely and put into a blender or mash it in a bowl. Add the garlic, onion, a large pinch of salt, paprika, and some of the lemon juice. Blend lightly and then add alternating small amounts of the tahini paste and remaining lemon juice. The final consistency should be thick and smooth. Adjust this and the seasoning with more salt, tahini, or lemon juice.

Turn into a serving bowl and garnish with the herbs and olives. Just before serving with pita bread or crudités, dribble the oil over the top.

Clockwise from the top left: Assorted Phyllo Pastry Parcels (page 16), Grape Leaves Stuffed with Seafood Mousse (page 17), Baba Ghanouj, baby eggplants, black olives, and Spicy Hummus with Tahini served with crudités

ASSORTED PHYLLO PASTRY PARCELS

MAKES ABOUT 48

1 lb phyllo pastry, thawed if frozen
olive oil, for greasing
salt and freshly ground black pepper
FOR THE CHEESE FILLING
½ lb feta cheese
2 tbsp finely chopped walnuts
2 tbsp minced fresh chervil or chives
1 extra large egg, separated
FOR THE SHRIMP FILLING
½ cup crab meat
2 garlic cloves, minced
2 scallions, minced
3 tbsp mayonnaise
2 tbsp minced fresh flat-leaf parsley
juice of 1 lemon
15 large cooked shrimp, shelled and deveined
FOR THE SAUSAGE FILLING
4 small chorizo sausages, cut across into quarters
2 tbsp minced fresh flat-leaf parsley
cayenne pepper

Preheat the oven to 375°F and grease 2 baking sheets with oil.

First make the fillings: For the cheese filling, crumble the cheese into a bowl and stir in the nuts, herbs, and the lightly beaten egg yolk. Season and add just enough lightly beaten egg white to give a mixture with a thick but spoonable consistency.

For the shrimp filling: In a bowl mix all the ingredients except the lemon juice and shrimp. Season and add just enough of the lemon juice to give a sharp flavor and a thick but spoonable consistency.

Remove the sheets of phyllo pastry from their package only 2 or 3 at a time; reseal the package and return to the refrigerator. Use a damp cloth to cover those sheets not being worked with at any given time to prevent their drying out.

For the shrimp purses: Cut out 45×4-inch squares of phyllo. Oil lightly. For each purse, arrange 3 squares on top of one another so that the corners form a star shape. Put the filling in the center, press a shrimp into it, and then pull up the edges and twist around to form a coinpurse. Make sure the pastry is not too tightly wrapped around the filling. Brush the outsides of the purses lightly all over with oil.

For the cheese triangles: Cut the phyllo in long strips about 3 inches wide and brush these lightly with oil. Place a generous spoonful of the cheese filling on one end of each strip about 1 inch from that end and slightly off-center. Lifting the corner of the end farther from the filling, fold the pastry in to cover it and form a triangle. Then fold this stuffed triangle on its side parallel to the short edge of the strip of pastry up and over on the strip. Next fold this triangle on its diagonal side over onto the strip of pastry. Continue until all the strip is used. Press the edges lightly to seal the triangle well, and brush the outside lightly with oil.

For the sausage "cigars": Cut the phyllo into the same long strips as for the cheese triangles and lightly oil them. Place a piece of sausage at one end parallel to the short ends, sprinkle with a little cayenne and some parsley, and simply roll up, tucking in the edges as you go. Brush the finished "cigars" lightly with oil.

Arrange on the baking sheets and bake until just golden, about 25 minutes. Serve hot or warm with cocktails or as part of a buffet meal.

GRAPE LEAVES STUFFED WITH SEAFOOD MOUSSE

MAKES 18

2 washed lemons
4 large garlic cloves
1 tbsp oil
1 onion, minced
2 tsp minced fresh gingerroot
2 tbsp minced bulb fennel
½ lb white fish fillets, skinned
1 celery stalk, chopped into small dice
3 tbsp minced fresh coriander (cilantro)
1 egg, separated
½ cup cooked rice
3 oz cooked shelled bay or tiny shrimp
3 oz canned shucked baby clams, drained
salt and freshly ground black pepper
about 24 large grape leaves
2 cups canned plum tomatoes, chopped
2 tbsp minced fresh flat-leaf parsley
1 tbsp tomato paste
lemon slices, for serving

Finely grate 1 teaspoon of zest from one of the lemons and squeeze the juice from both. Cut 1 of the garlic cloves into fine slivers and mince the rest.

Put the oil in a sauté pan over medium heat. Add the onion, three-quarters of the minced garlic, the ginger, and fennel and sauté until the onion is soft but not browned.

In a food processor, purée the fish, celery, coriander, egg yolk, grated lemon zest, half the lemon juice, and the sautéed mixture. Be careful not to over-process! Stir in the rice, shrimp, and clams. Season generously.

Beat the egg white to stiff peaks and then stir a spoonful into the stuffing to loosen it. Gently fold the remaining egg white into the mixture.

If using grape leaves preserved in brine, cover with boiling water, stir well, and let soak about 30 minutes. Drain and rinse with cold water. Repeat the process. If using fresh leaves, blanch about 15 minutes in boiling water and then drain well.

Arrange 18 of the best leaves (don't use any with holes or tears) with vein sides up. Put a generous spoonful of stuffing on each leaf, near its base. Roll up the leaf from the base, tucking in the sides as you go. Take care not to wrap the filling too tightly as it needs a little room to expand. Squeeze the parcel gently in the palm to secure it.

Line a large heavy-based saucepan with the remaining grape leaves and arrange the rolled leaves on them with the tips tucked underneath to keep them rolled during cooking. Combine the remaining lemon juice and minced garlic, tomatoes and their liquid, parsley, garlic slivers, and tomato paste. Season and pour over the parcels. Cover and simmer over very low heat 30 minutes.

Serve the stuffed grape leaves hot, with a little of the cooking juices and garnished with lemon slices.

VEGETABLES, SALADS, AND EGG DISHES

M ore than anything else, it is the extraordinary range of fresh vegetables – brought to perfect ripeness by weeks of glorious sunshine – that forms the basis of Mediterranean cooking. Their brilliant colors and full rich flavors are used to advantage in the many vegetable dishes, such as *ratatouille* and *caponata*, traditional all over the region. The abundant fresh herbs also contribute their freshness and aromatic subtlety, especially to salads. Eggs and cheeses, such as Parmesan, ricotta, mozzarella, feta, and goat cheese, are also often teamed with vegetables in baked dishes or salads to great effect.

Clockwise from the right: Zucchini Gratin (page 20), Grilled Vegetables with Lemon Dressing (page 21), Sweet Red Peppers Stuffed with Fennel (page 20), and more grilled vegetables

ZUCCHINI GRATIN

SERVES 4

3 tbsp oil
2 tbsp flour
salt and freshly ground black pepper
3 or 4 large zucchini, cut into thick sticks
1 onion, minced
2 garlic cloves, minced
2 cups canned plum tomatoes, chopped
2 tsp minced fresh flat-leaf parsley
juice of 1 lemon
2 tbsp dry bread crumbs
3 tbsp freshly grated Parmesan cheese

Preheat the oven to 475°F and lightly grease a gratin dish with 1 tablespoon of the oil.

Put the flour in a shallow bowl and season it well. Dust the zucchini sticks lightly in the seasoned flour.

In a large sauté pan, heat another tablespoon of oil over medium-high heat and sauté the zucchini sticks until lightly browned. Remove from the pan and set aside.

Put the remaining oil in the pan and sauté the onion and garlic in it until soft and just beginning to color. Stir in the tomatoes and most of the parsley, bring to a simmer, and adjust the seasoning. Remove from the heat.

Put half the cooked zucchini sticks in a layer in the bottom of the gratin dish and sprinkle with half the lemon juice.

Spoon the tomato mixture over this layer and then cover with the remaining zucchini. Press the layers down slightly. Drizzle over the remaining lemon juice and then sprinkle the top with a mixture of the bread crumbs and the grated Parmesan.

Bake until the top is golden brown, about 20 minutes. Sprinkle with the remaining parsley before serving.

RED SWEET PEPPERS STUFFED WITH FENNEL

SERVES 4

4 large, rectangular red sweet peppers (see below)
4 fennel bulbs (see below)
5 tbsp oil
2 onions, finely chopped
4 garlic cloves, minced
1 lb (2 cups) ricotta cheese
½ cup finely chopped pistachios
salt and freshly ground black pepper
2 cups canned plum tomatoes, chopped
1 tbsp tomato paste
1 tsp sugar
⅛ teaspoon cayenne pepper
1 tbsp minced fresh flat-leaf parsley

Buy peppers and fennel bulbs of a uniform size so that the trimmed fennel bulbs will just fit inside the halved peppers.

Preheat the oven to 350°F and grease a wide baking dish with 1 tablespoon of the oil.

Halve the fennel bulbs lengthwise and trim them, discarding the woody cores and reserving the leafy tops. Blanch the bulb halves 5 minutes in boiling water. Drain and pat dry. Halve the peppers lengthwise and remove all seeds and pith.

Heat 2 tablespoons of the oil in a frying pan over medium heat and sauté the onions and 3 of the garlic cloves until just translucent.

In a bowl, mix these into the ricotta together with the nuts and seasoning. Place 3 or 4 spoonfuls of this mixture in each of the pepper halves. Carefully place a blanched fennel bulb in each pepper half so that it sits in the cheese mixture. Add more mixture around the edges of each, if necessary, to fill. Carefully transfer them to the baking dish.

Mix the tomatoes and their liquid with ⅔ cup of warm water, the tomato paste, sugar, remaining garlic, the cayenne, parsley, and salt to taste. Pour this carefully around the peppers. Drizzle the remaining oil over the peppers, cover the dish, and bake until the cheese is bubbling and the vegetables are beginning to brown, 20–30 minutes.

Serve hot, with a little cooking liquid drizzled over them and garnished with the fennel sprigs.

GRILLED VEGETABLES WITH LEMON DRESSING

SERVES 4

3 large garlic cloves
8 tbsp extra virgin olive oil
2 small fennel bulbs
2 red sweet peppers
2 yellow sweet peppers
4 baby zucchini
4 plum tomatoes
2 red onions
1 eggplant
1 washed lemon
2 tbsp minced fresh flat-leaf parsley
salt and freshly ground black pepper

The day before cooking, halve the garlic cloves, put them into a bowl, and cover with the oil. Cover and let infuse in a cool place until needed. Remove and discard the pieces of garlic.

Halve all the vegetables lengthwise. Remove the cores from the fennel and the pith and seeds from the peppers. Cut the eggplant halves into large chunks.

Finely grate 1 teaspoon of lemon zest and squeeze the juice. Preheat a charcoal grill or the broiler.

Make the dressing: Mix 6 tablespoons of the flavored oil with 2 tablespoons of the lemon juice. Stir in the lemon zest and half the parsley. Season.

Arrange all the vegetables on the barbecue grill or in the broiler pan and brush generously with some

of the remaining oil. Grill until blistering on all sides, turning and brushing with more oil as necessary.

Transfer to a warmed serving platter and drizzle over the dressing. Sprinkle with remaining parsley.

NOTES: Baby corn can be added to the vegetables. The grilled vegetables look particularly attractive served on a bed of mixed green leaves, especially watercress and curly endive.

FATTOUSH

SERVES 4

2 large, flat pita breads
juice of 2 or 3 large lemons
1 bunch of scallions, thinly sliced
6 large, ripe tomatoes, chopped
1 English cucumber, diced
1 small green sweet pepper, seeded and finely diced
1 small red sweet pepper, seeded and finely diced
2 large garlic cloves, minced
8 tbsp olive oil
6 tbsp minced fresh flat-leaf parsley
3 tbsp finely chopped minced fresh coriander (cilantro)
3 tbsp minced fresh mint
salt and freshly ground black pepper
⅔ cup thick plain yogurt, for serving
pomegranate seeds, for garnish (optional)

Split open the pita breads and toast them lightly. Then break them into bite-size pieces.

In a bowl, toss the pieces of bread in the lemon juice, ensuring that they are all moistened.

Add the remaining ingredients and season to taste, adding more lemon juice if necessary.

Serve topped with a spoonful or two of yogurt and sprinkled with pomegranate seeds, if using.

NOTE: This is the traditional way of making this salad, but all the solid ingredients can simply be tossed in the lemon juice and oil at the last minute.

A Syrian peasant salad dish, FATTOUSH can cleverly use up slightly stale pita bread.

Sicilian CAPONATA, *like its close French relation, ratatouille, is served cold as an hors d'oeuvre or warm as a vegetable dish in the summer, traditionally piled in a dome shape.*

TABBOULEH, *a salad of bulghur wheat and herbs, originated in the mountains of Lebanon. The freshness of the parsley and mint perfectly balance the pungency of the raw onion and garlic to produce a dish that is uniquely refreshing. Cilantro leaves are also often included.*

CAPONATA

SERVES 4

2 eggplants, cut into ½-inch cubes
salt and freshly ground black pepper
16 canned anchovies, drained
about 3 tbsp olive oil
1 large onion, sliced
2 garlic cloves, minced
1 cup canned plum tomatoes, drained and chopped
1 bouquet garni
2 tbsp tomato paste
3 tbsp sherry vinegar or white wine vinegar
2 large zucchini, cut into large dice
1 large red sweet pepper, seeded and diced
1 large green sweet pepper, seeded and diced
⅓ cup capers, with a little of their liquid
2 or 3 celery stalks, thinly sliced
½ cup pitted black olives, cut into strips
2 tbsp minced fresh flat-leaf parsley

Put the eggplant cubes in a colander, sprinkle well with salt, and let drain about 15 minutes. Rinse well and pat dry. Rinse the anchovies in warm water, pat dry, and cut into strips.

Preheat the oven to 350°F and grease a large ovenproof casserole dish with a little of the oil.

Heat the remaining oil in a large pan and cook the onion over low heat until soft, 2–3 minutes. Add the garlic and cook 1 minute longer.

Stir in the tomatoes, bouquet garni, and tomato paste. Simmer until reduced to a thick purée, about 20 minutes. Discard the bouquet garni. Stir in the vinegar and simmer 1 more minute.

Mix the eggplants, zucchini, and peppers into the tomato purée together with the anchovies, capers, celery, and olives. Adjust the seasoning.

Spoon into the casserole, cover, and bake until all the vegetables are quite tender, about 1½ hours.

Serve warm or cool, sprinkled with parsley.

TABBOULEH

SERVES 4

1 cup bulghur wheat
6 tbsp olive oil
juice of 3 lemons
2 garlic cloves, minced
3 onions, minced
salt and freshly ground black pepper
small bunch of fresh mint
½ lb ripe juicy tomatoes, finely chopped
½ English cucumber, finely diced
large bunch of fresh flat-leaf parsley, minced
2 or 3 small scallions, chopped, for garnish
small romaine lettuce leaves, for serving

Put the bulghur in a large bowl and cover well with warm water. Let soak until soft and swollen, about 20 minutes. Drain thoroughly, squeezing to remove excess moisture, and place in a large serving bowl.

Mix the olive oil, two-thirds of the lemon juice, the garlic, and onions. Season to taste and pour this dressing over the bulghur. Stir well and let marinate at least 20 minutes.

Just before serving, mince the mint, reserving a few of the best small leaves for garnish. Mix the minced mint into the salad, together with most of the tomatoes, the cucumber, and parsley. Adjust the seasoning with more salt, pepper, and lemon juice as necessary (it should taste quite sharp).

Garnish with the remaining chopped tomatoes, the chopped scallions, and the reserved whole mint leaves. Serve with small romaine lettuce leaves to act as scoops.

Left: Tabbouleh; right: Provençal Vegetables with Goat Cheese (page 24)

SALADE NIÇOISE

SERVES 4

½ lb tiny fine green beans
½ lb tiny ripe tomatoes, cut into wedges
1 green sweet pepper, seeded and cut into strips
1 English cucumber, cut into thick strips
2 oz canned anchovies, drained
⅓ cup pitted black olives
7 oz canned tuna fish in oil, drained and flaked
4 hard-cooked eggs, shelled and quartered
5 tbsp olive oil
1 tbsp white wine vinegar
1 garlic clove, minced
salt and freshly ground black pepper
2 tbsp chopped fresh flat-leaf parsley

In its native South of France, SALADE NIÇOISE commonly also contains fava beans and artichokes. Elsewhere, lettuce and cooked potatoes are popular additions.

Blanch the beans briefly until just tender and refresh in cold running water. Pat dry.

Mix the vegetables in a large salad bowl (or arrange in separate piles around the bowl). Arrange the anchovies, olives, flaked tuna, and eggs over the top.

Make a dressing by vigorously mixing the oil, vinegar, and garlic with seasoning. Pour this over the salad and sprinkle with the parsley.

PROVENÇAL VEGETABLES WITH GOAT CHEESE

SERVES 4

1 small, round goat cheese, weighing about 2½ oz (see below)
¼ lb tiny broccoli florets
¼ lb fine green beans
¼ lb snow peas
2 small zucchini, cut into thick slices
2 large garlic cloves
4 tbsp olive oil
1 tbsp lemon juice
pinch of dried thyme
4 or 5 ripe juicy tomatoes, coarsely chopped
salt and freshly ground black pepper
2 scallions, minced
pine nuts, for garnish (optional)

Select a cheese that is firm but not too dry.

In a large pan of boiling salted water, blanch the vegetables in batches until just tender but still very firm to the bite: 6–7 minutes for the broccoli, 5 minutes for the beans, and 2–3 minutes for the snow peas and zucchini.

Drain each batch of vegetables promptly as they are ready and refresh them under cold running water. Drain well, pat dry, and let cool.

Make the dressing: Put the cheese, garlic, oil, lemon juice, and thyme in a blender or food processor. Mix until smooth.

Add the tomatoes in small batches, processing each until smooth. Add just enough to give the dressing a rich consistency that is thick but liquid enough to coat the vegetables. Season well.

Put the cooled vegetables in a large bowl and pour over the dressing. Toss well to coat all the ingredients thoroughly. Scatter over the scallions and garnish with pine nuts, if using.

SWEET PEPPER SALAD

SERVES 4

1 large red sweet pepper
1 large green sweet pepper
1 large yellow sweet pepper
18 pitted black olives
3 tbsp olive oil
juice of 1 large lemon
3 garlic cloves, minced
3 tbsp minced fresh flat-leaf parsley
salt and freshly ground black pepper

Preheat the broiler. Halve the peppers and remove their seeds and pith. Broil the pepper halves, skin-side up, until the skins are black and blistering.

Let cool a little and then peel them. Cut the flesh into strips and mix in a salad bowl or on a serving plate.

Finely chop half the olives and halve the others.

Make the dressing by mixing the oil, lemon juice, chopped olives, garlic, and half the parsley. Season generously with salt and pepper.

Drizzle the dressing over the peppers and toss well. Sprinkle the salad with the remaining parsley and dot with the olive halves. Serve warm or cold.

An optional extra is to add 5 ounces of bacon that has been fried until crisp, well drained, and crumbled.

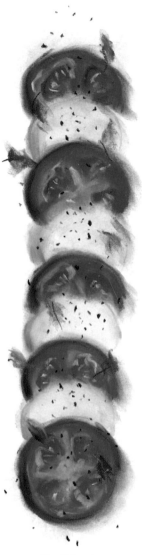

*Traditional tasty
mozzarella cheeses
made from buffalo
milk are now
available from
many specialty food
stores and Italian
grocers.*

MOZZARELLA AND TOMATO SALAD WITH AVOCADO

SERVES 4

*2 buffalo or fresh mozzarella cheeses, thinly sliced
2 beefsteak tomatoes, thinly sliced
small basil leaves, for garnish*
FOR THE AVOCADO DRESSING
*1 large ripe avocado
1 tbsp balsamic vinegar
1 large red onion, minced
4 tbsp olive oil
salt and freshly ground black pepper*

First make the dressing: Halve and pit the avocado and scoop the flesh into a bowl. Add the vinegar and mash the onion into the avocado flesh.

Gradually add the oil, mixing all the time, until it has all been incorporated. Season to taste.

On a serving plate, arrange the mozzarella and tomato slices in alternating rows. Drizzle dressing over the centers of the rows and garnish with basil.

SCRAMBLED EGGS WITH SWEET PEPPERS★

SERVES 4

*6 tbsp butter
1 tbsp vegetable or olive oil
1 green sweet pepper, seeded and cut into julienne strips
1 red sweet pepper, seeded and cut into julienne strips
2 garlic cloves, minced
pinch of dried thyme
2 tbsp balsamic vinegar
8 extra large eggs
(★see page 2 for advice on eggs)
salt and freshly ground black pepper
1 or 2 dashes of Worcestershire sauce
chopped fresh chives, for garnish*

In a large heavy frying pan, melt one-third of the butter with the oil over medium-low heat. Add the pepper strips, garlic, and thyme. Season and cook gently 2–3 minutes. Tip into a bowl and pour the vinegar over. Cover and keep warm.

Melt the remaining butter in the pan. Lightly beat the eggs with some seasoning and Worcestershire sauce. Pour into the pan and cook very gently, stirring all the time, until just becoming thick.

Serve immediately on warmed plates. Stir the pepper mixture and spoon some over the eggs. Sprinkle with chives.

NOTE: This dish can also be served on toast, or in hollowed-out baked bread croûtes, or even in blanched sweet pepper halves.

SWISS CHARD AND PINE NUT TART

SERVES 4

*2 tbsp butter
1 tbsp olive oil
1 onion, minced
2 large garlic cloves, minced
10 oz Swiss chard leaves
6 tbsp minced fresh flat-leaf parsley
juice of ½ lemon
salt and freshly ground black pepper
½ lb frozen pie pastry, thawed
2 eggs, beaten
½ cup pine nuts
⅔ cup crème fraîche or whipping cream
6 tbsp milk
pinch of freshly grated nutmeg
sun-dried tomatoes in oil, for garnish (optional)*

Preheat the oven to 350°F.

Melt the butter with the oil in a large sauté pan over medium heat. Sauté the onion and garlic until translucent and then add the Swiss chard, parsley, lemon juice, and some seasoning.

Sauté briefly over medium–high heat until the chard is softened. Set aside.

Roll out the pastry on a lightly floured surface and use it to line a 10-inch tart or quiche pan. Cover the bottom with foil and weight with dried beans.

Bake about 10 minutes and then remove the beans and foil. Return to the oven and bake until the pastry is firm but not yet brown, about 10 minutes longer. Brush with a little of the beaten egg and bake 5 minutes more.

While the tart shell is baking, toast all but 1 tablespoon of the pine nuts on a baking sheet until golden brown, 5–10 minutes.

In a bowl, mix the cream, milk, eggs, and nutmeg. Season and stir in the chard mixture. At the last minute, stir in the toasted pine nuts.

Pour into the pastry shell, scatter over the remaining pine nuts, and bake 20 minutes.

Garnish with chopped sun-dried tomatoes in oil, if desired.

NOTES: Spinach can be used instead of Swiss chard. Some chopped bacon or ham can be cooked with the chard for extra flavor.

Alternatively, for a delicious and unusual sweet tart, replace the onion, garlic, parsley, and seasoning with golden raisins, honey and a pinch of ground allspice.

TORTILLAS, *or Spanish omelettes, are a mainstay of the traditional selections of snacks enjoyed in tapas bars. They are served warm or cold, cut in thick wedges or squares.*

SALSA *is the Spanish and Italian word for sauce, but it is now commonly used in English for dressings spiced with chili.*

ZUCCHINI TORTILLA WITH HERB SALSA

SERVES 4–6

2 large potatoes, diced small
2 tbsp butter
2 tbsp olive oil
2 onions, minced
3 garlic cloves, minced
3 large zucchini, thinly sliced
salt and freshly ground black pepper
8 eggs, beaten
2 tbsp chopped fresh flat-leaf parsley
FOR THE HERB SALSA
5 tbsp olive oil
1 tbsp red wine vinegar
1 tsp whole-grain mustard
⅓ cup chopped canned plum tomatoes, drained
pinch of chili powder
2 tbsp each chopped fresh chives and flat-leaf parsley

In a large pan of boiling salted water, blanch the potato dice 2–3 minutes. Refresh under cold running water, drain well, and pat dry.

In a 10-inch frying or omelette pan, preferably with a lid, melt the butter with the oil over medium heat.

Sauté the onions and garlic until the onion is translucent and soft. Add the zucchini and potatoes and sauté a few minutes more, taking care that the onion and garlic do not get too brown.

Season the eggs and stir in most of the parsley. Stir into the pan, cover, and cook over low heat until the eggs are just set, about 10 minutes.

Meanwhile, preheat the broiler. Finish cooking the omelette under the broiler to brown the top.

While the tortilla is cooking, make the salsa by mixing all the ingredients and seasoning to taste.

Serve the tortilla warm or cold, sprinkled with the remaining parsley. Serve the salsa separately.

GORGONZOLA AND ANCHOVY SOUFFLÉ

SERVES 4

3 tbsp unsalted butter
2 oz canned anchovy fillets, drained
1 tbsp flour
⅔ cup milk
3 eggs, separated
3 oz gorgonzola cheese, crumbled or cubed
freshly ground black pepper
cayenne pepper

Preheat the oven to 375°F and heat a baking sheet in it. Grease a 6-inch soufflé dish with 1 tablespoon of the butter. Make sure that the rim is well greased to prevent the soufflé sticking as it rises.

Rinse the anchovies to remove excess saltiness, pat them dry, and cut them into small strips.

In a large heavy-based saucepan, melt the remaining butter over low heat and stir in the flour. Cook 1–2 minutes, stirring constantly. Gradually add the milk, still stirring, and cook until smooth and thick.

Off the heat, stir the egg yolks into the sauce, one at a time. Then stir in the cheese and anchovies. Adjust the seasoning with pepper and cayenne pepper (the seasoning should be quite forceful as it will be cut by the unseasoned egg white). Set aside.

Beat the egg whites to stiff peaks. Spoon a little of the beaten egg white into the cheese mixture and stir well to loosen the mixture. Carefully fold the remaining egg white into the mixture.

Pour the mixture into the prepared soufflé dish. Tap the base on a work surface, then put the dish in the oven on the hot baking sheet.

Bake until well risen and golden, 20–25 minutes. Serve immediately, dusted with cayenne.

Zucchini Tortilla with Herb Salsa

FISH, MEAT, AND POULTRY

The emphasis on vegetables and grains, together with the practice of composing meals of many small dishes, means that meat and poultry do not hold the same dominant position in Mediterranean kitchens as they do in ours. They are generally reserved for holidays, or seen much more as flavoring ingredients and used in wonderful combinations with rice, pasta, and vegetables, as in *moussaka* or kebabs. On the other hand, the Mediterranean peoples have always made much of the abundance of fish and seafood readily available to them, especially the nutritious and health-giving oily fish, such as mackerel, sardines, and tuna, served plainly grilled, stuffed with herbs, or blended into rich purées.

Top: Bouillabaisse with Rouille (page 32); Bottom: Baked Red Mullet with Rosemary (page 33)

Conger eel, gurnard, and the Mediterranean rascasse, or scorpion fish, are essential for an authentic version of the Provençal fish soup, BOUILLABAISSE, but any good selection of white and firm-fleshed fish will do. The soup must boil vigorously to emulsify the oil.

The spicy mayonnaise, ROUILLE, accompanies many fish dishes, especially soups. Traditionally, slices of bread are spread with a little rouille, placed in the bottom of deep bowls, and the broth ladled over.

BOUILLABAISSE WITH ROUILLE★

SERVES 6–8

2 1/4 lb mixed whole white fish, such as whiting, bass, haddock, cod, red mullet, monkfish, and red snapper
1 1/2 lb whole rich fish, such as striped bass, mackerel, and eel
1/2 lb mussels
3 onions
3 leeks
3 celery stalks
2 pinches of saffron
2 cups canned chopped plum tomatoes
4 garlic cloves, minced
1 bouquet garni
1/2 small fennel bulb, minced
thin strip of orange zest
bunch of fresh flat-leaf parsley
3/4 cup olive oil
salt and freshly ground black pepper
1 bay leaf
juice of 1/2 lemon
1 tbsp tomato paste
thick slices of country bread, toasted, for serving

FOR THE ROUILLE

4 garlic cloves, chopped
2 egg yolks
(★see page 2 for advice on eggs)
1 tsp cayenne pepper
6 tbsp olive oil
1–2 tbsp tomato paste

Make sure that the fish have been cleaned and scaled, if necessary. Cut all the fish into large chunks, reserving the heads and tails. Place the chunks in a large bowl, keeping the white and rich fishes separate. Scrub the mussel shells well and discard any that do not close on being tapped.

Cut one each of the onions, leeks, and celery stalks into large pieces; chop the remainder.

Soak the saffron in a few spoonfuls of warm water. Add half of it to the bowl of fish along with the chopped onions, leeks, and celery, the tomatoes, garlic, bouquet garni, fennel, orange zest, and two-thirds of the parsley, minced. Pour over the oil and season well. Cover and let marinate 1–2 hours in a cool place.

Meanwhile, place the fish heads and tails in a large pan. Add the vegetables that have been cut into large pieces, most of the remaining bunch of parsley, the bay leaf, and lemon juice and just cover with water. Season and bring to a simmer. Simmer 20 minutes and then strain.

Remove the pieces of fish from the marinade and set aside. Tip the marinade into a large saucepan. Add the strained fish stock and the remaining saffron and its water. Bring to a boil and simmer about 30 minutes.

While this cooks, make the rouille: Put the garlic and egg yolks in a food processor and add the cayenne and a tiny pinch of salt. Blend to a thick paste. With the machine running, add the oil in a thin steady stream as if making mayonnaise. The finished sauce should have a thick, creamy consistency. Color it with tomato paste and season with more salt and cayenne as necessary (it should be quite spicy).

Bring the simmering liquid to a rapid boil and add the chunks of rich fish and the prepared mussels. Continue to boil vigorously about 6 minutes and then add the white fish chunks. Continue to boil until the flesh of the white fish flakes readily, about 5 minutes longer. Transfer the fish and shellfish to a warmed serving dish, discarding any mussels that have failed to open. Remove the bouquet garni and orange zest from the broth and pour it into a warmed tureen. Add just enough tomato paste to give a good color and adjust the seasoning. Snip the remaining parsley over fish and broth for garnish.

BAKED RED MULLET WITH ROSEMARY

SERVES 4

4 tbsp olive oil
6 tbsp minced shallots
2 garlic cloves, minced
6 sprigs of fresh rosemary
1 cup dry white wine
4 small red mullet, cleaned, but with their livers retained
salt and freshly ground black pepper
juice of 1 lemon
2 tbsp minced fresh flat-leaf parsley
lemon wedges, for serving

Preheat the oven to 450°F and grease a baking dish with some of the oil.

Put the shallots and garlic in a saucepan with 2 rosemary sprigs, cut in half. Add all but 6 tablespoons of the wine and boil until reduced by about three-quarters, to leave the softened shallots and a sticky liquid. Discard the rosemary.

With a sharp knife, make some shallow cuts on both sides of the fish to allow the heat to penetrate. Slip a rosemary sprig into the cavity of each fish and season.

Spread the shallot mixture in the bottom of the baking dish, season, and arrange the fish on top, alternating heads and tails. Drizzle over the remaining oil and wine and bake 15 minutes, basting from time to time.

Sprinkle with the lemon juice and parsley and serve, accompanied by lemon wedges.

MARINATED SARDINES

SERVES 4

8 fresh sardines, cleaned and filleted
1 ¼ cups olive oil
1 large onion, thinly sliced
3 garlic cloves, minced
strip of washed orange zest
2 or 3 sprigs of fresh thyme
2 or 3 sprigs of fresh rosemary
1 bay leaf
juice of 2 lemons
salt and freshly ground black pepper
cayenne pepper
2 tbsp minced fresh flat-leaf parsley, for garnish
lemon wedges, for serving

Put the sardine fillets in a large sauté pan and add half the oil. Heat to a gentle simmer and cook until golden. Turn and cook the other sides in the same way. Transfer the sardines to a deep dish.

Mix the onion, garlic, orange zest, herbs, and lemon juice into the oil in the pan together with the remaining oil and 3 tablespoons of water. Season with salt, pepper, and a large pinch of cayenne.

Bring to a boil and simmer about 15 minutes. Let cool slightly, then pour the cooled mixture over the sardines. Let marinate overnight.

Garnish with the chopped parsley and serve with lemon wedges, crusty bread and a green salad.

RED MULLET *is a popular fish all around the Mediterranean. It isn't a true mullet, but is a member of the goatfish family. Red mullet is rarely available in the USA, except on the Gulf Coast, but you can prepare other fish with firm, lean flesh, such as red snapper, in the same way.*

BACCALÀ IN GOLDEN BREAD CROÛTES

SERVES 4

1 lb salt cod
4 thick slices from a square white loaf of bread
3 tbsp butter, melted
2 garlic cloves
⅞ cup olive oil
about ⅔ cup light cream, warmed
2 tsp walnut oil
1 tbsp lemon juice
pinch of grated nutmeg
salt and freshly ground black pepper
1 tbsp minced fresh flat-leaf parsley, for garnish
lemon wedges, for serving

BACCALÀ, *or salt cod, is popular in the cooking of many Mediterranean countries, from Spain and Portugal to Greece. The French have their own celebrated version of the fish, puréed with oil and milk, known as* brandade de morue. *Thorough soaking of the fish to remove excess saltiness is essential.*

Soak the salt cod 1 or 2 days, ideally under cold running water, to remove excess saltiness.

Drain the fish and put it in a large pan with cold water to cover. Cover, bring to a boil, and simmer very gently until just tender, 6–7 minutes.

Drain and let cool until it can be safely handled. Remove and discard all skin and bones and flake the flesh into a large bowl.

Preheat the oven to 350°F.

Trim out a deep hollow on one side of each slice of bread, taking care not to tear all the way through. Using a pastry brush, paint the pieces of hollowed-out bread all over with melted butter.

Bake the croûtes until a uniform golden color, 15–20 minutes. Remove from the oven and, while still warm, carefully rub them all over with one of the garlic cloves. Keep warm.

While the croûtes are baking, warm ⅔ cup of the oil in a heavy pan. When very hot, reduce the heat and add the fish. Using a wooden spoon, beat in the fish over very low heat.

When the mixture begins to be really mushy, mince the remaining garlic and stir it in. Transfer to a large mortar or food processor. Start adding the remaining oil and the warmed cream in alternating small amounts, pounding or blending in each addition thoroughly before adding any more. Do not over-process or the mixture will lose its texture.

The resulting purée should be smooth and stiff enough to hold a shape. Stir in the walnut oil, lemon juice, and nutmeg and season to taste.

Spoon the mixture into and around the croûtes. Sprinkle with the parsley and serve, accompanied by lemon wedges and a tomato salad.

BROILED SOLE WITH LEMON AND PARMESAN

SERVES 4

2 washed lemons
8 Dover sole fillets, skinned
salt and freshly ground black pepper
3 tbsp butter, melted
3 tbsp freshly grated Parmesan cheese
lemon wedges, for serving

Finely grate 1 tablespoon of zest from 1 of the lemons and squeeze the juice from both.

Rinse the sole fillets, pat them dry, and lay them in a shallow baking dish. Mix the lemon zest into the juice and season with a little salt and some pepper. Pour this over the fish and let marinate about 30 minutes, turning the fillets occasionally.

Preheat the broiler.

Remove the fish from the marinade. Arrange the fillets in the broiler pan and brush the tops with some butter. Broil 3–4 inches from the heat, about 5 minutes. Turn the fillets, brush the other sides with butter, and sprinkle with Parmesan. Broil until the cheese is melted and golden, 5–7 minutes longer.

Serve the sole immediately with the pan juices poured over them and with lemon wedges.

NEAPOLITAN STEAKS WITH PIZZAIOLA SAUCE

SERVES 4

2 tbsp olive oil
4 thick boneless sirloin steaks
salt and freshly ground black pepper
FOR THE PIZZAIOLA SAUCE
2 tbsp olive oil
2 onions, minced
4 garlic cloves, minced
1 small red sweet pepper, seeded and minced
1 1/2 lb very ripe tomatoes, chopped
1/8 teaspoon dried oregano
3 tbsp coarsely chopped fresh flat-leaf parsley
dash of hot pepper sauce

First make the sauce: Heat the oil in a saucepan and sauté the onions until lightly colored, 2–3 minutes. Add the garlic and minced red pepper and cook 1 minute more.

Add the tomatoes, oregano, and most of the parsley. Season with salt, pepper and hot pepper sauce. Cover and simmer over low heat about 15 minutes, stirring from time to time. The tomatoes should not become too pulpy.

Toward the end of this time, over medium-high heat, heat the oil in a large sauté pan that has a lid. Season the steaks and brown them rapidly on both sides.

Once the steaks are browned on both sides, reduce the heat to very low and pour the sauce over them. Cover and cook 3–7 minutes, depending on how well done you want the steaks to be. Adjust the seasoning if necessary.

Serve the steaks with the sauce poured over them and sprinkled with the reserved parsley.

NOTE: Try adding some chopped mushrooms to the sauce for extra flavor.

FRUIT AND NUT KOFTA

SERVES 4

2 tbsp butter
2 onions, minced
2 garlic cloves, minced
2/3 cup pine nuts
2 1/4 lb finely ground lean steak or lamb, or a mixture
3 or 4 dried apricots, minced
1/3 cup raisins
2 eggs, lightly beaten
pinch of ground allspice
salt and freshly ground black pepper
2 tbsp flour
2 tbsp freshly grated Parmesan cheese
2 tbsp olive oil
chopped fresh flat-leaf parsley, for garnish
lemon slices, for serving

Melt the butter in a large sauté pan over medium heat and sauté the onions, garlic, and pine nuts until just beginning to color.

Transfer these to a large bowl and knead together with the meat, fruit, eggs, allspice, salt, and pepper. Form into walnut-sized meatballs.

In a shallow plate, mix the flour and cheese and season well. Roll the meatballs in the mixture.

Heat the oil in the pan and sauté the meatballs over low heat until golden brown and cooked through.

Arrange in concentric circles on a warmed serving plate, garnish with parsley, and serve with lemon slices.

These meatballs are delicious served hot with a lemony yogurt or spicy tomato sauce and accompanied by rice or potatoes. They are equally good cold with salad, as part of a buffet or picnic.

A classic of Neapolitan cuisine, PIZZAIOLA is a rich and highly flavored tomato sauce used with meat and pasta.

KOFTA, or meatballs, are ubiquitous in Arab cooking, although they vary widely from place to place in their exact ingredients. They may even be shaped into fingers or flat cakes, like hamburgers. For the right texture the meat must be ground two or three times, or pulsed in a food processor until smooth.

YOGURT MOUSSAKA

SERVES 6–8

2 eggplants, thinly sliced
about ½ cup olive oil
¾ lb ground lean steak or lamb
4 large onions, thinly sliced
3 large garlic cloves, minced
3 tbsp minced fresh flat-leaf parsley
2 cups canned plum tomatoes, drained and chopped
⅓ cup tomato paste
2 eggs
2 cups thick plain yogurt
2 tbsp lemon juice
pinch of freshly grated nutmeg
½ cup freshly grated Parmesan cheese
salt and freshly ground black pepper

The Greeks claim MOUSSAKA *as their own dish, although the Turks adopted it and spread it throughout the Islamic world. This version uses yogurt and eggs instead of the more usual white sauce.*

Put the eggplant slices in a colander and sprinkle them generously with salt. Let drain about 30 minutes and then rinse thoroughly. Pat dry.

Heat 2 tablespoons of the oil in a large frying pan over medium heat and brown the eggplant slices in batches, draining them on paper towels as they are ready and adding more oil to the pan as needed.

Add 1 or 2 more tablespoons of the oil to the pan, increase the heat to high, and brown the meat: Spread it out into a flat cake and cook rapidly, undisturbed, until the underside is well colored. Then break up the cake, stir the meat well, and form it into a flat cake again. Cook in the same way. Repeat this process until the meat is a uniform color. Transfer to a bowl.

Heat 1 or 2 more tablespoons of the oil in the pan over medium heat and cook the onions until soft, 2–3 minutes. Add the garlic and parsley and cook for 1 minute or so longer. Add the tomatoes, browned meat, and tomato paste and simmer about 30 minutes. Season well.

Preheat the oven to 350°F and grease a deep baking dish generously with 1 tablespoon of the remaining oil.

Put a layer of one-third of the eggplant slices in the bottom of the prepared dish. Spoon over half the meat mixture and then repeat the layers, finishing with a layer of eggplant slices.

Mix the eggs into the yogurt and season with salt, pepper, lemon juice, and nutmeg. Pour this over the contents of the dish. Sprinkle Parmesan over the top and bake until golden brown, about 45 minutes.

NOTE: Try adding layers of sautéed mushrooms or zucchini, par-boiled potatoes or spinach, or slices of Gruyère cheese for extra interest. (You can then even omit the meat to make a vegetarian moussaka.) Add some red wine or 1 or 2 spoonfuls of brandy to the onions for extra flavor.

HONEYED LAMB KEBABS

SERVES 4

2 lb boned leg of lamb, cut into 1-inch cubes
4 onions, quartered
4 tomatoes, quartered
2 red sweet peppers, quartered and seeded
2 green sweet peppers, quartered and seeded
8 bay leaves
chopped fresh oregano or flat-leaf parsley, for garnish
lemon wedges, for serving

FOR THE HONEY MARINADE

1 washed lemon
¼ cup honey
6 tbsp olive oil
2 garlic cloves, minced
2 tbsp chopped fresh oregano
2 tsp crushed black peppercorns

First make the honey marinade: Finely grate 1 teaspoon of lemon zest and extract the lemon juice. Mix these with the remaining ingredients in a bowl. Add the pieces of lamb and onion quarters and stir well to coat them thoroughly. Cover and let marinate 2–3 hours in a cool place, stirring occasionally.

Preheat a hot grill, broiler or barbecue. Drain the lamb and onion well and thread on skewers, interleaved with pieces of tomato, pepper, and bay leaves. Grill until well browned on all sides, basting with the marinade from time to time.

Garnish with chopped oregano and serve with lemon wedges. A green or tomato and onion salad makes an excellent accompaniment.

NOTE: Add rolled bacon slices or quartered mushrooms to the kebabs for extra interest. Try replacing the oregano with mint, rosemary, or basil.

Clockwise from the top: Fruit and Nut Kofta (page 35) with a lemon-yogurt sauce, Honeyed Lamb Kebabs with a spicy tomato sauce, and Chicken Drumsticks with Garlic and Lime (page 39)

*Calves' liver must
not be over-cooked
or it loses its
delicate texture.
Try to get it sliced
as thinly as possible
and cook very
briefly over
medium-high heat.*

ROAST LAMB IN A GARLIC-CUMIN CRUST

SERVES 4

*6 large garlic cloves
1 leg of lamb, weighing about 3½ lb
2 tbsp cumin seeds
3 tbsp olive oil
salt and freshly ground black pepper*

Thinly slice 2 of the garlic cloves and chop the others. About 1 or 2 hours ahead of time, with the tip of a sharp knife make deep incisions in the meat of the leg of lamb and insert the slices of garlic into them. Let the lamb absorb the flavor of the garlic.

Preheat the oven to 375°F.

Crush the cumin seeds in a mortar with a pestle and then add the chopped garlic and continue pounding to make a thick paste. Season well with salt and pepper and then start adding the oil a little at a time, to make a smooth paste with a good spreading consistency.

Brush this all over the lamb. Put the lamb on a rack in a roasting pan and roast about 1½–2 hours, depending on how well done you want the lamb to be.

Remove from the oven, cover with foil, and let rest in a warm place at least 10 minutes before carving.

NOTE: This dish is particularly good when cooked in a covered barbecue kettle.

Serve with baked potatoes and sautéed zucchini shreds or eggplant fritters.

CALVES' LIVER WITH SAGE AND LEMON

SERVES 4

¼ cup flour
salt and freshly ground black pepper
8 very thin slices of calves' liver, each weighing
about 2 oz
small bunch of fresh sage
4 tbsp butter
1 tbsp olive oil
3 large onions, thinly sliced
1 garlic clove, minced
dash of sherry or red wine vinegar
juice of 1 large lemon

Put the flour in a shallow dish and season it with salt and pepper. Lightly dredge the slices of liver in it. Cut most of the sage leaves into thin strips, reserving some of the best-looking sprigs for garnish.

Melt the butter with the oil in a large sauté pan over medium heat. Add the onions, garlic, and half the chopped sage to the pan and cook until soft, 5–10 minutes. Then turn up the heat, season, and add the sherry vinegar. Sauté until just beginning to caramelize.

Using a slotted spoon, transfer the onions to a warmed serving dish. Keep warm.

Cook the slices of liver in the pan over medium-high heat, in batches if necessary, 2–3 minutes on each side. Transfer to the serving dish, cover, and keep warm as they are cooked.

Deglaze the pan with the lemon juice, stirring to scrape up any browned bits. Add the remaining chopped sage and cook 1 minute or so.

Arrange the liver slices sitting atop mounds of the onion on 4 warmed plates. Pour over the sauce and garnish with the reserved sage sprigs.

CHICKEN DRUMSTICKS WITH GARLIC AND LIME

SERVES 4

3 garlic cloves, minced
2 tbsp olive oil
4 limes
salt and freshly ground black pepper
12 chicken drumsticks, preferably from free-range birds
cayenne pepper, for garnish

Mix together the garlic, olive oil, and the juice of 3 of the limes in a large bowl and season well. Add the chicken pieces and mix them in so that they are well coated. Cover and let marinate in the refrigerator several hours, turning from time to time.

Preheat the oven to 400°F.

Drain the drumsticks and arrange in a baking dish. Bake until browned and the juices run clear when the thickest part is pierced, about 30 minutes.

While the chicken is cooking, pour the marinade into a saucepan and boil it until reduced to a sticky sauce-like consistency. Adjust the seasoning (according to preference, the tartness may also be cut slightly with a little sugar).

Serve the drumsticks dusted lightly with cayenne, with the remaining lime cut into wedges and the sauce in a bowl for dipping.

The marinated chicken drumsticks are also delicious barbecued. Brush them liberally with the marinade several times during cooking. For a really economical but tasty dish, use chicken wings.

MOROCCAN LEMON CHICKEN

SERVES 4

4 washed lemons
1 free-range chicken, weighing about 3½ lb,
giblets retained
2 onions
1 bay leaf
1 tsp black peppercorns
3 tbsp minced fresh flat-leaf parsley
1 tbsp olive oil
1 tsp minced fresh gingerroot
pinch of ground cinnamon
salt and freshly ground black pepper
3 tbsp minced fresh coriander (cilantro)

Preheat the oven to 425°F.

Grate 1 tablespoon of zest from the lemons and pare off 2 or 3 thin strips of zest. Quarter 2 of the other lemons.

Trim the giblets, removing any dark bits, and put in a small pan with 1 of the onions, the bay leaf, peppercorns, the strips of lemon zest, and any stems from the parsley. Cover with water, bring to a boil, and simmer gently about 1 hour. Strain and reserve.

Finely chop the remaining onion. Heat the oil in a sauté pan over medium heat and sauté the onion, together with the grated lemon zest, ginger, cinnamon, and seasoning until soft.

Transfer to a bowl and mix in most of the chopped parsley and coriander. Stuff the chicken with this mixture and the lemon quarters, squashing them lightly as you insert them.

Place the chicken in a roasting pan, breast down. Add just enough water to cover the bottom of the pan and roast for about 50–60 minutes, turning over halfway through and basting regularly, until well browned all over and the juices run clear when the thickest part of the thigh is pierced.

Transfer the chicken to a warmed serving platter, tipping it so that any liquid inside the bird drains back into the pan. Garnish with one of the remaining lemons, cut into wedges, and the remaining herbs.

Deglaze the roasting pan with the juice from the last of the lemons, scraping up any browned bits with a wooden spoon, and boil briefly to reduce to a sticky liquid. Add the giblet stock and boil to reduce to a sauce-like consistency. Adjust the seasoning and serve this sauce separately, adding any juices that run from the chicken during carving.

In North Africa, this dish would be made using lemons that have been dried or preserved in oil, giving a much more pungent flavor.

The ancient Persian FAISINJAN *sauce of pomegranates and walnuts was used mostly for wild duck and other game birds, but suits chicken and domestic duck. If fresh pomegranates are unavailable, use 2 or 3 tablespoons of pomegranate syrup mixed with 1¼ cups of water instead of the strained juice, but do not add sugar.*

RABBIT WITH PRUNES, OLIVES, AND BACON

SERVES 4

1 large rabbit, cut into pieces
¼ lb pitted prunes, halved
2 tbsp oil
1 tbsp flour
1¼ cups red wine
1¼ cups chicken stock
2 garlic cloves, minced
1 bouquet garni
salt and freshly ground black pepper
5 oz bacon, cut into strips
½ cup pitted black olives, halved

FOR THE MARINADE

1¼ cups red wine
2 tbsp oil
1 large onion, coarsely chopped
1 large carrot, coarsely chopped
12 black peppercorns
1 bay leaf

Mix the marinade ingredients in a bowl and add the rabbit and prunes. Stir well, cover, and let marinate in a cool place 2–3 hours, stirring occasionally.

Remove the rabbit, prunes, and vegetables from the marinade and pat dry. Heat the oil in a Dutch oven over medium heat and brown the rabbit in it. Remove the rabbit and brown the vegetables. Sprinkle over the flour and sauté about 1 minute.

Stir in the marinade, wine, and stock together with the garlic, bouquet garni, and seasoning. Return the rabbit pieces to the pot. Bring to a boil, cover, and simmer gently about 30 minutes.

Toward the end of this time, fry the bacon until brown. Add it, the olives, and prunes to the pot and cook 15 minutes more. Transfer rabbit, prunes, olives, and bacon to a serving dish. Boil the juices rapidly to reduce to a sauce.

DUCK BREAST FAISINJAN

SERVES 4

4 pomegranates
juice of 1 large lemon
1 tbsp light brown sugar or honey
salt and freshly ground black pepper
4 boned duck breast halves
1 tbsp olive oil
1 onion, minced
¾ cup chopped walnuts

Halve the pomegranates and scoop the seeds into a food processor, reserving 2 or 3 tablespoons. Blend briefly and then press through a strainer.

Put this juice into a pan and add half its volume of water, the lemon juice, sugar, and season. Bring to a boil and simmer gently about 20 minutes. Cool.

Prepare the duck breasts by making several diagonal cuts through the fat to the meat.

Put the duck breasts in a bowl and pour over the cooled pomegranate mixture. Stir well, cover, and let marinate 2–3 hours.

Preheat the broiler. Drain the duck breasts, reserving the marinade. Pat them dry and broil fat side up until well browned, 5–8 minutes. Turn and cook the other side in the same way. (Duck is best served fairly pink; if you prefer it well done, reduce the heat and cook another 10 minutes or so.)

While the duck is cooking, heat the oil in a saucepan over medium heat and add the onion and walnuts. Cook until the onion is soft, 2–3 minutes. Add the pomegranate mixture to the saucepan, bring to a boil, and simmer about 5 minutes. Adjust the seasoning and the sweet-and-sour balance with more lemon juice or sugar.

Serve the duck thickly sliced, sprinkled with the reserved seeds. Pass the sauce separately.

Duck Breast Faisinjan garnished with watercress

RICE, GRAINS, AND PASTA

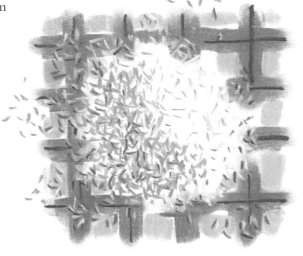

Perhaps the peak of creativity in Mediterranean cooking is reached in their clever ways of using staples like rice and grains. Scarcely ever served as mere plain accompaniments, they are cooked slowly with flavoring ingredients to make dishes as splendid as *risotto*, *paella*, and *lasagne*. Less common grains such as couscous, polenta, and bulghur wheat are also cooked with rich sauces or made into refreshing salads. The versatility of pasta has been most people's first glimpse of this amazing inventiveness. The myriad different pasta shapes available can be combined with literally innumerable sauces to make anything from light snacks to substantial meals – and even interesting desserts.

Saffron Paella (page 46) with an array of rice, pasta, legumes, and flavoring ingredients

There are endless variations on the Spanish rice dish, PAELLA – only rice, oil, and saffron are essential. Other ingredients may include green beans, green peas, and artichoke hearts, lobster, duck, and rabbit.

SAFFRON PAELLA

SERVES 6–8

1 chicken, weighing about 3 lb, cut into 12 pieces, backbone and giblets retained
4 onions
3 large garlic cloves, chopped
white part of 1 leek, chopped
1 celery stalk, thinly sliced
1 bouquet garni
12 black peppercorns
salt and freshly ground black pepper
¾ lb squid, sliced into rings
about 18 mussels
¼ cup olive oil
½ lb chorizo sausage, sliced
1 large red sweet pepper, seeded and cut into thick strips
1 large green sweet pepper, seeded and cut into thick strips
few strands of saffron
6 large tomatoes, peeled and chopped
cayenne pepper
2 cups long-grain rice
6–8 jumbo shrimp or any large prawns (optional)
lemon wedges, for serving

Put the chicken giblets and backbone in a pot with 2 of the onions coarsely chopped, the garlic, leek, celery, bouquet garni, peppercorns, and a large pinch of salt. Barely cover with water and bring to a boil. Skim and then simmer about 1 hour.

Meanwhile, put the squid in a pan and cover with cold water. Bring to a boil and simmer 5 minutes, then drain and set aside. Scrub the mussel shells well, discarding any open ones that do not close when tapped. Finely chop the remaining onions.

Heat the oil in a large frying or paella pan over medium heat and brown the chicken pieces. Remove them with a slotted spoon and set aside.

In the same oil, cook the chorizo, squid, pepper strips, and chopped onions 3–4 minutes. Stir in the saffron and cook 5 minutes longer. Add the tomatoes and bring to a boil. Season well and add 1–2 pinches of cayenne.

Stir in the rice. Place the chicken pieces, mussels, and prawns, if using, on top. Pour in the strained chicken stock and bring to a boil.

Cover and simmer gently until the rice is tender, about 20 minutes. Keep checking; if it looks too dry, add a little water. Serve with lemon wedges.

SALAMI AND BLUE CHEESE RISOTTO

SERVES 4

3 tbsp butter
2 tbsp olive oil
1 large onion, minced
2 large garlic cloves, minced
1 ½ cups risotto rice, preferably arborio
3¾–4 cups hot chicken or veal stock
½ lb Italian salami, peeled and cubed
½ lb gorgonzola or other blue cheese
2 celery stalks, chopped
1 large red sweet pepper, seeded and cut into thin strips
⅛ teaspoon dried sage
2 tbsp minced fresh flat-leaf parsley
salt and freshly ground black pepper
cayenne pepper
chopped fresh chives, for garnish

In a large heavy pan that has a tight-fitting lid, melt the butter with the oil over medium heat. Add the onion and garlic. Cook until soft and just beginning to color 1–2 minutes.

Add the rice and sauté over medium-high heat for 2 minutes. Add 1¼ cups of stock, stir well, and bring to a boil. Reduce the heat and simmer gently until the stock is absorbed, about 5 minutes.

Continue to add the remaining stock, one-quarter at a time, stirring well and waiting until it has all been absorbed before adding more. The whole process should take about 30 minutes and the final result should be rice that is richly creamy and slightly sticky – but not mushy.

About halfway through, add half the salami and cheese with the celery, red pepper, and sage.

With the final addition of stock, add the remainder of the salami and cheese and the parsley. Adjust the seasoning with salt, pepper, and cayenne. Serve garnished with chives.

CHICKEN AND LAMB COUSCOUS

SERVES 6–8

2 tbsp oil
1 large chicken, cut into 12 pieces, backbone retained
½ lb boned lamb, cut into large cubes
3 onions, chopped
4 garlic cloves, minced
3 turnips, cut into chunks
3 large carrots, chopped
salt and freshly ground black pepper
few strands of saffron
½ tsp each of ground cumin, ginger, and turmeric
4 large ripe tomatoes, chopped
4 zucchini, chopped
½ cup raisins
bunch of fresh flat-leaf parsley, minced
bunch of fresh cilantro, minced
1 cup canned chickpeas (garbanzos), drained
1 lb (2⅔ cups) instant couscous
2 tsp harissa or other chili sauce
2 tbsp butter
2–3 tbsp rose water
⅓ cup dates, cut into slivers
more harissa sauce, for serving

In the bottom part of a couscoussier or a large heavy saucepan, heat the oil over medium-high heat and brown the pieces of chicken and lamb.

Add the onions, garlic, turnips, carrots, and the chicken backbone. Cover with water, season, and stir in the saffron and other spices. Bring to a boil and simmer about 1 hour, skimming as necessary.

Remove and discard the backbone. Add the tomatoes, zucchini, raisins, most of the herbs, and two-thirds of the chickpeas. Simmer 30 minutes more.

Prepare the couscous either by simply pouring boiling water over it, letting it steep about 10 minutes, and draining it, or by steaming it about 20 minutes in the top part of the couscoussier.

Remove 2 ladlesful of the broth and season it with the harissa. When the couscous is fluffed up and ready, stir in one-third of this seasoned broth along with the butter, the remaining chickpeas, the rose water, and dates.

Serve the couscous on a large warmed serving platter with the pieces of meat and vegetables piled in the center and some of the broth poured over. Sprinkle with the remaining herbs and pass the remaining seasoned broth and more harissa separately.

Fiery-hot HARISSA SAUCE *from Tunisia can be bought in Middle-Eastern grocers.*

LENTIL AND BULGHUR PILAF WITH YOGURT

SERVES 4

1 cup + 3 tbsp green lentils, preferably le Puy
1 bay leaf
1 tsp cumin seeds, finely crushed
1 tsp coriander seeds, finely crushed
1 1/3 cups bulghur wheat
pinch of cayenne
salt and freshly ground black pepper
6 tbsp olive oil
2 onions, thinly sliced
2 garlic cloves, minced
juice of 1/2 lemon
2/3 cup thick plain yogurt
2 tbsp minced fresh cilantro

Soak the lentils in cold water about 1 hour. Drain and put them in a pan. Pour in 5 cups of fresh water and add the bay leaf and spices. Bring to a boil and simmer until just tender, about 20 minutes.

Remove the bay leaf and add the bulghur wheat with the cayenne and seasoning to taste. Stir well, cover, and remove from the heat. Let sit until the bulghur is tender, about 20 minutes. Check from time to time to see if it has become too dry and add a little more water as necessary.

Meanwhile, heat one-third of the oil in a frying pan over medium heat and cook the onion and garlic until brown and just beginning to caramelize.

Transfer the lentil and bulghur mixture to a warmed serving dish. Drizzle over the remaining oil and top with the onion and garlic mixture. Stir the lemon juice into the yogurt and pour it over the middle. Sprinkle the dish with the cilantro.

Serve hot, warm, or cold, with a green salad.

Top: Chicken and Lamb Couscous (page 47); bottom: Lentil and Bulghur Pilaf with Yogurt

GAME LASAGNE

SERVES 4–6

2 large partridges or other game birds
1 lb apples, peeled, cored, and thickly sliced
1¼ cups dry hard cider
1¼ cups game consommé
9 tbsp butter
¼ cup flour
1¾ cups milk
⅔ cup light cream
2 cups sharp grated Cheddar cheese
salt and freshly ground black pepper
1 tsp ground allspice
1 tbsp vegetable or olive oil
about 1 lb fresh lasagne, preferably a mixture of colors
¼ cup freshly grated Parmesan cheese

Preheat the oven to 375°F.

Put the birds in a roasting pan with the apples, cider, and consommé. Cover with foil and bake 20 minutes. Remove from the oven and let cool.

When the birds are cool enough to handle, remove all the meat and slice it thinly. Using a slotted spoon, transfer the apples to a bowl and reserve the cooking liquid.

Heat a large pot of water for the lasagne.

Melt 4 tablespoons of the butter in a saucepan over medium heat. Sprinkle in 2 tablespoons of flour and cook 1–2 minutes, stirring constantly. Gradually add the milk, stirring to make a smooth liquid. Bring nearly to a boil, still stirring, and simmer gently until thickened. Stir in the cream and Cheddar and continue to stir until the cheese has melted. Season.

In another pan make another sauce as above, starting with 4 tablespoons of the remaining butter and the remaining flour, but adding about 1½ cups of the reserved game cooking liquid instead of milk.

Season with salt, pepper, and allspice. Stir in the apples.

When the pasta water is boiling rapidly, add 2 tablespoons of salt and the oil. Drop in the lasagne, bring back to a rolling boil, and cook until just tender but still very firm to the bite. Drain and drop into a bowl of cold water.

Grease a large baking dish with the remaining butter. Spoon some cheese sauce over the bottom and arrange some of the drained lasagne over that. Layer some partridge meat over the lasagne and spoon some game sauce and apples over that. Continue layering in this way, finishing with cheese sauce.

Sprinkle with Parmesan and bake until bubbling and well browned on top, about 30 minutes.

TAGLIATELLE WITH ROAST GARLIC

SERVES 4

about 30 large garlic cloves, preferably the fresh summer
variety, unpeeled
1 bay leaf
6 tbsp olive oil
⅔ cup pine nuts
salt and freshly ground black pepper
1 lb dried tagliatelle
small bunch of fresh basil leaves
1 tbsp balsamic vinegar
freshly grated Parmesan cheese, for serving

Preheat the oven to 425°F.

Put the garlic cloves and bay leaf in the center of a large sheet of foil. Add 2 tablespoons of oil, wrap in a loose package, and put in a baking dish.

Bake until the garlic is tender but not mushy, about 20 minutes. About halfway through, add the pine nuts to the oven, scattered on a baking sheet.

Meanwhile, put about 4½ quarts of water in a pasta pan or large pot. Add 2 tablespoons of salt and 1 tablespoon of oil and bring to a boil.

When the water is boiling rapidly, put the pasta in and bring it back to a rolling boil as quickly as possible. Boil rapidly, uncovered, until the pasta is tender but still firm, testing regularly.

Remove the foil package and toasted pine nuts from the oven. Take the garlic from the foil and let cool slightly. Squeeze the cloves out of their skins, first snipping off one end if necessary. Keep the pine nuts and garlic cloves warm. Finely chop most of the basil, reserving 12 small leaves.

As soon as the pasta is ready, drain well and stir in the remaining oil with most of the garlic and pine nuts, the chopped basil, vinegar, and seasoning. Dot the remaining garlic, pine nuts, and basil leaves over the top. Serve accompanied by Parmesan.

The delicious Italian fresh double-cream cheese, MASCARPONE, is available in Italian markets and specialty food stores. More usually served with sugar or fruit at the end of a meal, its subtle flavor and buttery texture are also incomparable in savory dishes.

PASTA SHELLS WITH MASCARPONE AND NUTS★

SERVES 4

6 oz (¾ cup) mascarpone cheese
2 tbsp butter, melted
1 tbsp balsamic vinegar
½ tsp freshly grated nutmeg
salt and freshly ground black pepper
1 lb pasta shells
1 tbsp olive oil
2 egg yolks
(★see page 2 for advice on eggs)
½ cup freshly grated Parmesan cheese
¾ cup coarsely chopped walnuts

Put the mascarpone in a large serving bowl and stir in the butter, vinegar, half of the nutmeg, and seasoning. Set in a warm place in the kitchen.

Cook the pasta in boiling salted and oiled water as described for the tagliatelle (left). While the pasta is cooking, in another large bowl lightly beat the egg yolks with half the Parmesan and season.

Drain the pasta quickly so that some water still clings to it and immediately stir it well into the egg mixture. The egg should cook on contact.

While the pasta is still very hot, add it to the cheese mixture together with two-thirds of the walnuts and toss to coat uniformly.

Sprinkle over the remaining walnuts, Parmesan, and nutmeg, and serve.

Clockwise from the top: Tagliatelle with Roast Garlic; Pasta Shells with Mascarpone and Nuts; Spaghettini with Chicken and Eggplant (page 52)

Throughout Italy, many types of PASTICCIO, or pasta pies, are served on special occasions. Usually topped with a pastry lid, they can be filled with a wide variety of types of pasta and other ingredients, including eggplant, ricotta cheese, and pigeon.

SPAGHETTINI WITH CHICKEN AND EGGPLANT

SERVES 4

1 large eggplant, cut into ½-inch cubes
6 tbsp olive oil
1 onion, minced
4 garlic cloves, minced
¼ lb chicken breast meat, cut into ½-inch cubes
about 30 pitted black olives
2 cups canned plum tomatoes, chopped
salt and freshly ground black pepper
pinch of sugar
1–2 tbsp tomato paste
1 lb dried spaghettini
chopped fresh basil, parsley, or tarragon, for garnish

First make the sauce: Sprinkle the eggplant with salt and let drain in a colander about 20 minutes. Rinse well and pat dry.

Heat 2 tablespoons of oil in a sauté pan over medium heat and cook the onion 1–2 minutes. Add the garlic and cook 1 minute more. Using a slotted spoon, transfer the onion and garlic to a bowl.

Add the cubes of chicken to the pan and sauté them briskly, until beginning to brown, 1–2 minutes. Transfer to the bowl.

Add 2 more tablespoons of oil to the pan and sauté the eggplant until browned.

Halve some olives for garnish and chop the rest.

Return the chicken, garlic, and onion to the pan along with the chopped olives and the tomatoes with their liquid. Season and add the sugar. Simmer gently about 10 minutes. It should be a good thick sauce: Adjust the consistency with some tomato paste, as necessary.

Meanwhile, cook the pasta in boiling salted and oiled water until just tender but still firm to the bite, as described for the tagliatelle (page 50).

Stir 1 tablespoon of oil into the cooked and drained pasta and pour the sauce over it. Garnish with the halved olives and the herbs.

NOTE: Add some chopped cooked ham or bacon or a spoonful of brandy when sautéing the chicken, for more flavor. This dish is also good for vegetarians without the chicken. Sprinkle with some shredded mozzarella cheese to make it more substantial.

OPEN PASTICCIO WITH CHICKEN LIVERS

SERVES 6

FOR THE PASTRY
2 cups flour
10 tbsp butter, softened
2 tbsp butter, for greasing
FOR THE FILLING
1 lb tagliatelle, preferably a mixture of colors
7 tbsp olive oil
salt and freshly ground black pepper
1 large onion, minced
3 garlic cloves, minced
3 oz chicken livers, trimmed
3 tbsp Marsala or sweet sherry wine
⅔ cup crème fraîche or heavy whipping cream
¼ lb frozen spinach leaves, thawed and squeezed dry
⅛ teaspoon freshly grated nutmeg
1 buffalo mozzarella cheese
2 tbsp freshly grated Parmesan cheese

To make the pastry dough: Sift the flour with a pinch of salt and rub the butter into it gently with your fingertips. When it has a crumb-like consistency, add enough cold water, a little at a time, to make a smooth dough. Roll into a ball and chill 1 hour. Roll out the dough to a thickness of about ½ inch and fold it in thirds. Roll out and repeat this process twice more and then roll back into a ball and chill 30 minutes more.

Preheat the oven to 425°F and generously grease a deep 9-inch round spring form pan with butter. Roll out the dough and use to line the mold.

To make the filling: Cook the pasta in boiling salted and oiled water as for tagliatelle (page 50), but stop cooking when just slightly underdone. Drain thoroughly. Stir in 2 tablespoons of oil and season.

While the pasta is cooking, heat 2 tablespoons of the remaining oil in a sauté pan over medium heat and sauté the onion 2–3 minutes. Add the garlic and cook 1 minute more. Then add the chicken livers, and as soon as these change color, add the Marsala or sherry. Sauté 1 minute more. Stir in the cream and season. Set aside. Season the spinach with salt, pepper, and nutmeg.

Arrange a layer of half the tagliatelle in the bottom of the pastry shell, so that there is a depression in the middle. Pour the chicken liver mixture into the center. Arrange half the mozzarella slices on top and then cover these with half the spinach. Put half the remaining tagliatelle on top of this, followed by layers of the remaining mozzarella, spinach, and tagliatelle. Sprinkle over the remaining oil and the Parmesan.

Bake until the pastry is firm and the top golden, 30–35 minutes. Let cool 2–3 minutes before removing from the mold.

Top: Open Pasticcio with Chicken Livers; bottom: Mozzarella and Tomato Salad with Avocado (page 26)

DESSERTS

*L*ike most Mediterranean food, the desserts of the region reflect the glories of the local produce. With such an abundance of luscious fruits like melons, apricots, citrus fruits, figs, and grapes, flavorful nuts such as walnuts, almonds, and pistachios, rich aromatic blossom honeys, and the wide range of delicious and refreshing fresh cheeses and yogurt, there has never really been much place for elaborate creamy cakes in the Mediterranean kitchen. Even the pâtisserie of the region makes inspired use of paper-thin phyllo pastry to produce confections, such as baklava, that are at once richly satisfying but yet at the same time lighter and healthier than most of our more familiar and heavier pies, gâteaux and pastries.

Top: Yogurt, Date, and Honey Cheesecake (page 57);
bottom: Tarte au Citron (page 56)

French lemon tart, Tarte au Citron, is one of the glories of Provençal cooking. The riper and more fragrant the lemons, the better the filling will taste. Make an orange or tangerine tart in the same way, using 3 large juicy oranges or 8 tangerines in place of the lemons and adding 1 tablespoon of grated zest to the pastry.

TARTE AU CITRON

SERVES 6–8

1 ⅔ cups flour, plus more for dusting
¾ cup confectioners' sugar, plus more for dusting
1 stick/8 tbsp butter, softened, plus more for greasing
4 eggs
pinch of salt
few drops of vanilla extract
5 washed lemons
½ cup granulated sugar
⅔ cup finely ground almonds
⅔ cup whipping cream

Sift the flour and confectioners' sugar into a bowl and work the butter in lightly with your fingertips. Make a well in the center and add 1 of the eggs, the salt, vanilla, and the grated zest of 1 lemon. Gradually bring the flour in from the edges and mix to a smooth dough. Chill the dough about 30 minutes.

Preheat the oven to 350°F and grease a 10-inch loose-bottomed tart pan with butter.

Roll out the dough on a lightly floured surface and use it to line the pan. Do not remove any overhang. Chill briefly until firm.

Line with foil or wax paper, weight with dried beans, and place on a baking sheet. Bake about 10 minutes. Remove from the oven, take off weights and paper and trim the edges. Return to the oven and bake 10 minutes longer.

Meanwhile, finely grate the zest of 2 of the remaining lemons and extract the juice from all the lemons. In a large bowl, beat the remaining eggs with the granulated sugar until thick enough to form a ribbon trail. Stir in the lemon zest and juice, together with the almonds and cream.

Pour this filling into the baked pastry shell as soon as it comes from the oven. Return to the hot baking sheet in the oven and bake 30 minutes.

Preheat the broiler. Sprinkle the top of the tart liberally with sifted confectioners' sugar and flash under the broiler to caramelize it. Serve hot or warm.

ORANGE AND ALMOND RICE PUDDING

SERVES 6

1 tbsp butter
¾ cup short-grain rice
nearly 1 cup sliced almonds
7 tbsp sugar
1 quart milk
finely grated zest and juice of 2 large washed oranges
juice of 1 small lemon
⅔ cup crème fraîche or heavy whipping cream
⅛ teaspoon ground cinnamon
1 tbsp orange flower water, rum, or orange liqueur
(optional)

Preheat the oven to 350°F and grease a large baking dish with the butter. Rinse the rice thoroughly and finely crush half the almonds.

Put the rice, sugar, milk, and orange zest in a large pan and bring to a boil, stirring constantly.

Immediately transfer to the prepared baking dish and stir in the crushed almonds, orange juice, lemon juice, cream, cinnamon, and orange flower water, rum, or liqueur, if using.

Bake about 1 hour, until the rice is tender, stirring from time to time during the first 30 minutes.

About three-quarters of the way through, spread the remaining almonds on a baking sheet and put them in the oven to toast lightly.

Serve the rice pudding with the toasted almonds sprinkled on top, along with a little more cinnamon.

YOGURT, DATE, AND HONEY CHEESECAKE

SERVES 8–12

3 tbsp butter, melted
6 sheets of phyllo pastry
1 ¼ cups thick plain yogurt
6 tbsp skim milk
3 tbsp rice or potato flour
⅓ cup ground almonds
⅓ cup mild-flavored honey
1 cup ricotta cheese
3 eggs, lightly beaten
⅓ cup raisins
⅓ cup chopped dates
grated zest and juice of 1 small washed lemon
grated zest and juice of 1 small washed orange
2 tbsp orange flower water or almond liqueur
confectioners' sugar, to finish

Preheat the oven to 375°F and grease a 10-inch loose-bottomed tart pan with some of the butter.

Trim the sheets of phyllo so that they are about 12-inches square. Line the pan with them, brushing each with butter and putting it at an angle of about 60 degrees to that beneath it to fan out the corners.

Mix the yogurt and milk in a large pan and sift in the flour. Then add the almonds and honey. Bring almost to a boil, stirring constantly. The mixture should become quite thick. Let cool slightly.

Transfer to a large mixing bowl and add the cheese and all but 1 tablespoon of the beaten eggs. Beat in well. Stir in most of the fruit, reserving some for decoration, together with the citrus zest and juice and the orange flower water or liqueur.

Pour into the pastry shell, brush the top lightly with the reserved beaten egg, and bake for about 45 minutes, or until a good light golden brown.

Dust with confectioners' sugar and decorate with the reserved fruit before serving.

TIRAMISÙ★

SERVES 6–8

12 ladyfinger cookies
1 tsp instant coffee
2 tbsp brandy
2 tbsp Marsala wine
3 eggs, separated
(★see page 2 for advice on eggs)
3 tbsp sugar
¾ lb (1 ½ cups) mascarpone cheese
3 oz semisweet chocolate

Cut the ladyfingers in half lengthwise. Line the bottom of a deep glass serving bowl with half the ladyfingers, cut side uppermost.

Dissolve the coffee in 2 tablespoons of boiling water and mix the brandy and Marsala into it. Use a pastry brush to paint the ladyfingers with this.

Beat the egg yolks with the sugar until the mixture is thick and pale. Then beat the cheese into this mixture a spoonful at a time.

Beat the egg whites until standing in stiff peaks and fold into the cheese mixture.

Grate half the chocolate into tiny pieces. Spread half the cheese mixture over the ladyfingers and sprinkle with half of the chocolate pieces. Repeat the layers.

Finish by smoothing the top of the cheese mixture and chill at least 4 hours or overnight.

Just before serving, grate the remaining chocolate finely over the top. Use within 24 hours.

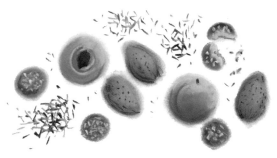

The Italian coffee-flavored dessert, TIRAMISÙ, has become a great restaurant favorite in recent years. It often disappoints, however, having been made with custard rather than thick, rich mascarpone cheese. For more flavor and crunch, spread the layers of ladyfingers with some apricot preserves and stud the top with tiny amarettini cookies.

58

MARINATED MELON FILLED WITH FRUIT

SERVES 6–8

1 large cantaloupe
1 small ripe mango
3 oz sweet grapes, preferably muscat
¾ lb (about 3–4 cups) mixed summer fruit, including
sweet cherries, raspberries, strawberries,
and red currants
2 tbsp lemon juice
1 tbsp rose or orange flower water
2 tbsp kirsch, maraschino or Grand Marnier
2–3 tbsp sugar
small pinch of salt

Cut a thin slice off the base of the melon so that it will sit stably. Cut a "lid" off the top. Scoop out and discard the seeds. Then scoop out the flesh with a melon baller or spoon, taking care not to pierce the skin.

Peel the mango and chop the flesh into pieces the same size as the pieces of melon. Reserving a few on their stalks for decoration, remove the seeds from the grapes if necessary and halve if large.

Mix the melon flesh with the prepared mango and grapes and half the summer fruit. Mix the lemon juice, rose or orange flower water, and 1 tablespoon of liqueur and stir in all but 1 tablespoon of the sugar and the salt until dissolved. Use to dress the fruit, tossing gently to coat well. Let macerate in the refrigerator at least 2 hours.

Dissolve the remaining sugar in the remaining liqueur and swirl this mixture around the inside of the melon shell. Put the "lid" back on the melon shell and chill with the other fruit.

Just before serving, pile the fruit mixture into the chilled melon shell along with the macerating juices. Arrange the remaining summer fruit so that it spills decoratively from the top.

Melon shells make a delightful way of serving a whole range of dishes in summer. Make ice-cream using the mashed melon flesh mixed with 5 beaten egg yolks and 7 tbsp sugar. Stir the mixture over low heat until thick and then fold in 2 cups whipped cream. Flavor with lemon or lime juice and port wine, if desired. Freeze in an ice-cream machine. Pile into the well-chilled melon shell, and serve with fruit or raspberry purée. Alternatively, mix the melon flesh with citrus sections and chopped fresh mint or chunks of avocado, apples, and grapes. Dress with a light vinaigrette made with lemon or lime juice and serve in the melon shells as a refreshing first course.

PISTACHIO BAKLAVA

MAKES ABOUT 40 PIECES

1 stick butter, melted
½ cup blanched almonds
½ cup walnut pieces
15 sheets of phyllo pastry
2 cups chopped pistachios
1 tbsp sugar
½ tsp ground cinnamon
FOR THE SYRUP
2¼ cups sugar
1 cinnamon stick, broken into pieces
1 tbsp mild-flavored honey
2 whole cloves
½ tsp finely grated lemon zest
juice from ½ small washed lemon
2 tbsp orange flower water

First make the syrup: Mix all the ingredients except the orange flower water with 1 cup water in a saucepan. Place over medium heat and stir until the sugar has dissolved. Then bring to a boil and boil, without stirring, until the syrup is slightly thickened, about 4 minutes. Discard the spices and stir in the orange flower water. Let cool and then chill.

Preheat the oven to 325°F and grease the bottom and sides of a deep 8-inch square cake pan generously with some of the melted butter.

Toast the almonds either on a baking sheet in the oven as it warms or in a frying pan. Put them in a food processor or mortar with the walnuts and grind to the consistency of small bread crumbs.

Cut the sheets of pastry roughly to fit the pan. Layer 3 sheets in the bottom of the pan, brushing each with butter and trimming as necessary. Keep the other sheets covered with a damp cloth.

Mix together the pistachios, ground nuts, sugar, and cinnamon. Sprinkle one-quarter of this mixture over the pastry base in the pan.

Continue with layers of buttered phyllo and nuts until all are used up, finishing with a layer of 3 sheets of pastry. Brush this well with butter and sprinkle the top with 1 tablespoon of water.

Bake 45 minutes, then increase the heat to 425°F and continue baking until the baklava is puffed and lightly golden, 10–15 minutes longer.

As soon as the baklava comes out of the oven, pour the chilled syrup all over it. Let cool in the pan.

Slice in diagonal cuts about 2 inches apart and then do the same at right angles to cut the baklava into diamond-shaped pieces for serving.

COFFEE GRANITA

SERVES 4

6 oz dark-roasted coffee beans, ground
7 tbsp sugar
2 tbsp coffee liqueur, such as Kahlùa or Tia Maria
(optional)
light cream, for serving
candy coffee beans, for decoration (optional)

Put the coffee and sugar in a pot or large pitcher and pour in 5 cups of boiling water. Stir, cover, and let infuse in a warm place about 30 minutes.

Stir again and strain through a strainer lined with cheesecloth or a coffee filter paper.

Stir in the liqueur, if using, and freeze the mixture in a mold or ice cube trays 3–4 hours, without stirring.

Serve topped with a little cream and decorated with a few candy coffee beans.

NOTE: This is very refreshing and not too sweet; those with a sweet tooth may like to add more sugar to the freezing mixture.

Left: Pistachio Baklava; right: Zabaglione Ice-cream (page 63) with fresh raspberries

The Middle-Eastern nut pastry cake, BAKLAVA, is made with a mixture of almonds, walnuts, and pistachios. Here the pistachios predominate, but the nuts may be mixed in any proportion. It is important that the nuts are not ground too finely.

GRANITAS are Italian ices in which the formation of crystals is encouraged to give a refreshing grainy texture.

ZABAGLIONE ICE-CREAM★

SERVES 6

12 egg yolks
(★see page 2 for advice on eggs)
9 tbsp sugar
1¼ cups Marsala wine
1¼ cups whipping cream
fresh strawberries, raspberries, or chopped toasted
hazelnuts, for decoration

In a bowl, beat the egg yolks with the sugar until pale and thick. Stir in the Marsala and mix well.

Set the bowl over a saucepan of just simmering water. Stir constantly until the custard begins to thicken. Immediately remove from the heat and set the base of the bowl in cold water to stop the cooking, still stirring constantly. Let cool completely.

Whip the cream until standing in soft peaks and fold in the custard.

Freeze for about 6 hours in ice trays in the freezer, taking out and stirring vigorously with a fork halfway through to break up any ice crystals that have formed. Use within 48 hours.

Serve in tall elegant sundae glasses, decorated with fruit or nuts.

NOTE: This is a very rich ice-cream, but you can lighten it by adding the stiffly beaten whites of 2 or 3 of the eggs to the mixture.

BAKED FIGS STUFFED WITH WALNUTS

SERVES 4

12 ripe fresh figs
2 oz walnut halves
3 tbsp mild-flavored honey or light brown sugar
3 tbsp Madeira or sweet sherry wine
½ cup cream cheese

Preheat the oven to 400°F.

Cut a tiny slice off the base of each fig so that it will sit stably. Make 2 cuts down through their tops, about 1-inch deep, at right angles to one another. Ease the figs open with a spoon, squeezing their middles at the same time, if necessary.

In a food processor or mortar, grind most of the walnut halves coarsely, reserving the better-looking pieces for decoration. Do not over-process.

In a bowl mix the honey or sugar, Madeira or sherry, and ground nuts into the cream cheese. Spoon this into the opened figs and arrange them in a baking dish. Bake until the cheese is bubbling, 15–20 minutes. Arrange the reserved walnut halves on the tops of the figs and serve.

NOTE: Toasted almonds or hazelnuts work equally well in this dish, as does mascarpone cheese.

ZABAGLIONE *is a frothy Italian custard made from egg yolks beaten with sugar and alcohol. Usually served hot in tall glasses, it is most commonly flavored with Marsala, but some versions use sparkling white wine or even liqueurs.*

Baked Figs Stuffed with Walnuts

INDEX

ACKNOWLEDGMENTS
The Author would like to thank, Marie-Pierre Moine for her advice and encouragement and humbly acknowledges a great debt to the inspirational scholarly work of Claudia Roden and the late Elizabeth David. Also Judith Wills for opening his eyes to the nutritional wisdom of his favorite food.